W9-DFR-986

THE BANK BOOK

Edward F. Mrkvicka, JR.

THE BANK BOOK

Second Edition

HarperPerennial
A Division of HarperCollins*Publishers*

FIRST EDITION

Designed by Alma Orenstein

Library of Congress Cataloging-in-Publication Data

Mrkvicka, Edward F.
    The bank book / Edward F. Mrkvicka, Jr. — 2nd ed.
      p. cm.
ISBN 0-06-271520-8 — ISBN 0-06-273052-5 (pbk.)
1. Banks and banking—United States—Customer services.
  I. Title.
    HG1616.C87M74   1991
    332.1'0973—dc20   90-55993

91 92 93 94 95 CC/MB 10 9 8 7 6 5 4 3 2 1
91 92 93 94 95 CC/MB 10 9 8 7 6 5 4 3 2 1 (pbk.)

*This book is dedicated
to the loving memory of
Edward F. "Babe" Mrkvicka*

Acknowledgments

I would like to thank the entire staff of our newsletter, *Money Insider,* for their help and dedication, which culminated in this book.

Contents

Introduction

I have the highest regard for the banking system. Without it our economy as we know it today could not exist. What I have no respect for, however, are banks and bankers that prostitute the system for their own aggrandizement. Unfortunately, those types have taken over. That's why banks no longer meet the moral imperative of their banking charters. That's why bankers devise ways to deny banking services to the less affluent. That's why the Federal Deposit Insurance Corporation has reported that a substantial number of forced bank closings are the result of illegal insider transactions. That's why the cost of banking services continues to escalate while the quality of service continues to decline.

It might be different if banks competed for our business, but that's not the case. Banking competition is nonexistent. That's why all banks have the same prime interest rates. That's why they all have similar service charges. That's why you and I—if we had the time, money, and inclination, and even if we could offer the banking customer twice the service at half the price—cannot go out and start a bank. We would first have to be approved by either the state or federal government, subsequently by the FDIC. It's a closed club. With deregulation the club's membership is becoming smaller and smaller, to the detriment of the consumer.

The banking system has lost touch with reality. Why? Because it doesn't have to play by the rules. Through their exceptionally strong lobby group (the American Bankers Association), financial institutions have a very cozy relationship with Congress, the very Congress that should, through agencies, be supervising and regulating the system that allows the banks to flourish and profit. Let me give you one quick example to show the results of bankers' power. Congress, through the tax laws, has allotted banks unheard of concessions that have allowed banks as an industry to pay a yearly tax obligation of approximately 2.5 percent. Think about that! Here is an industry that earns billions and pays virtually no tax. This is just one example of the problem.

I have no objection to banks making money. In fact, they have an obligation to their shareholders to return a fair rate on their investments. But I take exception to the fact that much of the money they make is through deception, withholding of information, and planned intimidation. Banks function according to the principle that "you can make the most money from the people who can afford it the least" (meaning the average family).

How does that affect you? My own experience and research over the last twenty years indicates that you will overpay your bank, through mortgages, credit cards, loans, checking and savings accounts, over *$100,000* during your lifetime! Why? Because while you're trusting the bank and your banker, they're busy helping themselves to your finances. Education can stop your banker in his tracks. That's what this book offers. I am going to show you how and why the banks are ripping you off, and then, more importantly, I am going to show you how to fight back.

In 1969 I started working at a bank as a teller. By 1976, at age thirty-one, I was the president of a national bank in Illinois. I mention that for only one reason. You should judge my words by my record and by the facts. Although my banking career was most successful, I left the industry because it became clear that the system was not going to change. I decided that I was obligated at least to make my knowledge available to you, the consumer, so you can make intelligent financial decisions, decisions that could save you tens of thousands of dollars.

Banks are not to be trusted. My career experiences brought me to that conclusion. For instance, the banker who taught me consumer loans spent half the educational effort trying to convince me that customers needed to be abused "so they don't cause trouble." He wanted me to make each loan customer wait a minimum of fifteen minutes whether I was busy or not, so I would have the upper hand in the interview. The bank designed loan and other forms to be difficult, if not impossible, to understand. That way the bank would be protected in any legal dispute. Is this meeting the needs of the community? I thought not then, and I think not now. As my career progressed, it became more and more obvious that this abusive attitude toward the consumer was almost universal throughout the system.

Banks are not your friends. In truth, most should be sued for false advertising. Their ads say how much they want to help, and yet in the back room they are deciding the best way to take as much of your money as possible.

Should any reader think I am being too hard on the industry I ask you to reserve judgment. Read *The Bank Book* and then I think you'll understand my point of view. In fact, you're going to be mad! You're going to be outraged that you've lost so much money to your "friendly" banker. You're going to realize that you've done without, or maybe your children have done without, because you got robbed. And it wasn't done at gunpoint. It was done by a guy in a pinstriped suit, who smiled all the while. To me it doesn't matter how or why you were robbed. The result is just the same. In fact, in terms of money, you're better off being robbed on the street corner. That may only cost you a couple of hundred dollars. Your banker is going to cost you tens of thousands!

There are good banks and bankers, but they're in the vast minority. If by chance you have an institution that cares about its community, stick with it, and support them with all your business. However, before you make that judgment, read all of this book. You may find out your good bank is just another bad one.

The inherent nature of the banking system and the excesses of some bankers forced me to a disillusioning conclusion: *Banks are your financial enemy.* After reading this book, I challenge you to come to any other verdict.

THE BANK BOOK

General Principles of Credit

Obtaining Credit

Financial success is usually predicated on either having money or being able to obtain it. Often, being able to borrow money is the start of eventually having it. For this reason, understanding how your financial institution arrives at an answer to your loan requests is the first step to successful, intelligent, profitable borrowing.

The core of any loan decision should be the Five Cs of credit: character, capacity, capital, collateral, and conditions. Your bank obtains this information in a variety of ways—directly from you in the application and loan interview process, and through a credit check. Before exploring how the bank specifically obtains this information, let's review the banker's Five Cs: what they are, how they are applied, and how they *should* be applied.

Character

This should be, and historically was, the most important of the Five Cs. An applicant with unquestionable character was often approved for a loan that otherwise might be rejected. Character, from the banker's point of view, is most often obtained from a credit report. In a small town it may be determined by reputation or family ties.

The critical criterion is your payment record. Specifically your payment record with this bank. This is one reason, although you want to shop around for loans, to use the same financial institution again and again. Of course, I am assuming you are comfortable with a particular bank's rates and services.

Capacity

Capacity in this context is simply a measure of your finances. Successful people receive a high score. Others do not.

Capital

This is the amount of money you have at your disposal. It measures financial stability. It also gives the bank an idea of your ability to repay the debt.

Collateral

Collateral is the bank's insurance policy on your loan. It can't make a bad loan good, but it can make a good loan better. Collateral alone, without cash flow to pay the monthly expense, will not be enough to ensure loan approval. However, a slight deficiency in one area of your loan request might be offset by additional collateral if it's available.

Conditions

Condition considerations are usually reserved for business loan requests. For example, during a recession it would probably not be prudent for a bank to be loaning money for marginal new business ventures. The economic conditions of the moment would obviously have a negative impact on the loan request, regardless of the loan's actual merit.

For the individual customer, even though conditions don't usually affect the consumer per se, they may have a real effect on the loan officer's state of mind, which effect is then subconsciously passed on.

That's the way I learned the Five Cs some twenty years ago. Today, unfortunately, the Five Cs of credit have been reduced to Three Cs. Capital, collateral, and conditions.

Bankers' greed is the reason for the reduction of the Five Cs of credit. There was a time when a community bank's loan thrust was to the individual borrower. Those days are gone. The big borrower is what the banks are looking for, because they involve less servicing expense, and that means more net profit for the bank. For example, a million-dollar commercial credit is the equal to one hundred auto loans at $10,000 each. A billion-dollar credit is worth twenty thousand mortgage loans at $50,000 each.

With this profit mania in mind, let's review the Three Cs of credit as they are probably practiced at your local bank.

Capital

Capital, in the new banker's thinking, means: If you have $100 deposited in the banker's bank he is more than willing to loan you $50. It's an extension of the modern banker's credo: "If you don't need the money we're more than willing to lend it to you."

What the banks really want is to loan huge sums of money to large corporations that are already financially liquid, stable, and profitable. In their eyes, that is the safest loan possible. That is a misplaced value judgment.

Banks as an industry have failed to see that their real, dependable market is the individual depositor. Without such customers, the banker has no bank. Consequently, those customers' lending needs should be met. Granted, it's easier to service a large commercial loan, but all those fancy corporate financial statements offered as loan collateral aren't necessarily worth the paper they're printed on. If that weren't the case, why the record number of corporate bankruptcies? Think of what that kind of charge-off (loss) does to the bank's financial statement!

Regardless, because of the bank's attitude, you must convey the image of not really needing to borrow the money. You have to convey affluence. You need to legitimately, and legally, enhance your personal financial statement (as discussed later). Convincing the loan officer that you actually don't need the loan is absolutely necessary for quick loan approval and subsequent loan rate negotiations.

Collateral

Collateral should have no bearing on the loan officer's decision. The loan should stand or fall on its own merit. However, bankers like to feel secure, so they'll demand more and more collateral until they think they have a risk-free loan. Use caution.

Good loan officers know that cash flow and personal character are far more important than collateral. Repossessed collateral can be worthless. It can be "lost" or destroyed. It can be worth only nickels on the dollar. Despite these facts, most loan officers will demand excessive collateralization.

A home mortgage is a good example of present excessive collateral requirements. Typically the bank wants a 20 to 30 percent down payment. On a $100,000 home that means the bank, through the mortgage agreement, has a $20,000 to $30,000 equity cushion in case of default. Additionally, homes generally appreciate. Therefore, the bank's position improves each and every year, as the mortgage balance goes down while the property's value goes up. In short, this is a bank's safest loan. Yet home mortgage rates continue to be in excess of the bank's actual exposure to risk.

The need, in the banker's mind, for excessive collateral is another reason you must continually convince the bank that you are not just another customer. Image cultivation will grant you special consideration others will not receive.

Once you develop a profitable relationship with your loan officer, you can then use your collateral for interest rate reductions. Most customers offer collateral as an inducement for loan approval. Educated customers have created a financial persona that by itself will merit a positive response. Then they offer collateral in exchange for a lower interest rate.

If you don't learn how to play your collateral card, your collateral will at best help get the loan, nothing more.

Conditions

In tough times good banks excel and make more money than ever, while the marginal, poorly managed banks flounder. Hence the record bank closings. In 1990 alone, 169 banks were closed—that's one every 1.54 business days. Yet many banks reported record profits.

This interesting paradox gives the wise consumer excellent lending opportunities. If you have established yourself in the marketplace you will always have access to money. Your rates may escalate, but you'll be able to get money. This is important as some of the best investment opportunities are during those times when the average consumer couldn't borrow a dime if his or her life depended on it. If you've convinced the bank that they need you more than you need them you will be able to avail yourself of this critical fact of financial life; there is always money to be borrowed—the only question is, who gets to borrow it? You want to spend time and effort ensuring that the answer to that question is you.

One of the great lessons of the Depression, which seems to have been forgotten, is that while many fortunes were lost, many fortunes were made. Those who had access to money were in the driver's seat. They bought valuable assets for pennies on the dollar.

This has been true throughout history, yet most people ignore it. The economy is cyclical. Those prepared for that fact will reap the benefits. That's why you have to cultivate your lending relationship with a number of banks, and be ready to take advantage of conditions.

The Bottom Line

The final step in the credit decision is the credit check.

In order to ensure borrowing success I strongly recommend that you write to your local credit bureau and ask to see your file, before your banker does.

You have a legal right to see your credit file at any time.

The bureau does have the authority to charge a fair fee for that service, so don't be surprised if there is a nominal cost assessed.

Many credit bureaus are unreliable due to the crushing

volume of data they process. Mistakes are made daily. Erroneous data may be on your history, and that could cost you your loan. The most common problem is that, without urging from the consumer, bureaus quite often forget to note credit disputes on a file. These can show up as nonpayments and ruin your rating.

Obviously you want to make sure the credit bureau doesn't report any wrong information to your bank regarding your credit history. More important, if there is some bad news on the report, even correct information, you can lessen the impact at the bank. If there is a late payment, for instance, you can tell the loan officer that you had a problem that will probably show up on your credit report, but it was a disputed charge you legitimately refused to pay. The point of this "head 'em off at the pass" approach is that the banker will be impressed with your honesty. In short, you have taken a real negative and turned it into a positive.

If the credit bureau has made a mistake on your account, let them know that you expect it to be cleared immediately. They will comply, because if you're denied credit due to their error, you can file suit, under the Fair Credit Reporting Act, to collect damages. They know that, so they are willing to respond to an aggressive consumer.

Today, bankers rely on only three criteria in making credit decisions: capital, collateral, and conditions. Understanding the credit decision and how it works is a key to beating the system.

Do I Really Need to Borrow?

Borrowing money can be an expensive proposition, especially if you borrow when you don't need to.

Quite simply, you should never borrow for depreciating assets (assets that decrease in value with the passage of time).

You should borrow for things that you have to have, necessities, like housing. Borrow for your business. Borrow to make money (investments). Borrow when the cost of borrowing is less than the predictable inflationary increase of the purchase (example: when inflation was at 15 percent and mortgages were at 9 percent), providing a built-in profit maker. These are reasons to borrow. You shouldn't borrow for vacations, TV sets, and other luxury items. Why? Because you're never going to get ahead or stay even paying more for things than they're actually worth, that is, over and above retail or resale value. This small tip can save you thousands of dollars throughout your financial lifetime. Has your banker ever told you this sobering fact? Probably not. More likely he was more than willing to finance depreciating asset purchases at a high interest installment loan rate.

From Whom Should I Borrow?

Generally speaking, you should never finance a purchase through the seller of a product. Most of us will be tempted to do so when we buy a car. The dealer will tell you that he will arrange financing, do the paperwork, process the application, etc., and you won't have to do any legwork or be inconvenienced. Many salesmen will tell you that this is the best financing available because it comes "directly from the bank."

What the salesman won't tell you is that, although the bank will finance the loan, the car dealer will get a kickback from the bank at your expense. How does this work? Very simply, if your rate should have been 9 percent you will be quoted a rate of one to three percentage points higher, because you're dealing through a middleman. The difference goes to the dealer without your knowledge. A $10,000 car loan for forty-eight months could cost you $1,200 over and above what the bank would have quoted you, had you gone to the bank on your own.

Finance companies get their money from banks or investors, and then reloan the same money to the consumer. That's why it's so expensive to borrow from finance companies. They pass on their cost of borrowing and add to it their profit margin. There is also a greed factor involved, because the finance companies know that people who borrow from them don't understand the system or have no other way to borrow money. Obviously, you should never borrow from a finance company.

No matter who or what is involved you should never allow anyone to arrange your financing. You can't afford it!

Despite their disadvantages, banks are a constant source of credit, and one you should consider as an option. The problem is that banks use a very unfair lending form for most consumer loans. It's called an installment loan.

Installment Loans

Once you know your loan has been approved and you're satisfied with the interest rate, you must pay attention to the actual conditions of the loan. The most common type of personal loan offered to individual bank customers is the *installment loan.* An installment loan is a loan whereby the customer pays a portion of the value of the loan each month until the amount owed is completely payed. Not surprisingly, it is the most unfavorable. If at all possible, *you should never borrow on an installment loan basis.*

Let's look at a car loan where the car has a value of $9,000 and you make a down payment of $2,000. That leaves you with a balance of $7,000. I will use an example interest rate of 16.79 annual percentage rate (APR). A 16.79% APR is the use-of-money equivalent to a 9.5 add-on-rate. (Note: This example rate was chosen as representational of most market conditions.)

Sample Car Loan
16.79 APR for 48 months

Principal	$7,000.00
Credit life insurance	275.87
Disability insurance	413.81
Amount financed	7,689.68
Finance charge	2,920.72
Total due	$10,610.40
Monthly payments	$221.05

These are the conditions that your bank is most likely to offer you. Your banker will not give you alternatives, just this one "option," because it garners the bank its best return.

Let's go back. Remembering that the cost of the car was $9,000, we can see the real cost exceeds the original value by $3,610.40 (loan total of $10,610.40 plus our down payment of $2,000 minus the price tag of $9,000). Not a very good way of amassing a net worth, is it! It is important for you to think in terms of the total transaction.

The question now becomes, how can you improve this loan position and save money in the process? First of all, *never buy credit life and disability insurance from the lender*. This is discussed in depth later. I included these in the example because virtually all banks will write the insurance into the loan contract regardless of your wants and needs. Let's rewrite the example deleting those charges.

Sample Car Loan

16.79 APR for 48 months

Principal	$ 7,000.00
Credit life insurance	.00
Disability insurance	.00
Amount financed	7,000.00
Finance charge	2,660.00
Total due	$9,660.00
Monthly payments	$201.25

We've saved you nearly $20 a month or about $950 over the whole term of the loan. But there are more savings in store.

Front-End Loading

The borrower should never forget that installment loans are *front-end loaded,* that is, you are charged the add-on interest rate times the original balance throughout the term of the loan. Many borrowers are confused on this point; they believe that at the halfway point of the loan that they are paying interest on only 50 percent of what was borrowed. That isn't true. You are paying interest, in our example loan for instance, on $7,000 *for each and every month!*

Why isn't there a decreasing correlation of the interest rate and the declining balance? Because banks are more than willing to increase their profits at your expense. They are happy to arrange financing that isn't understood by the customer. Most of us rely on the bank or banker to help us with our lending needs, but unfortunately this is when the banker acts to his advantage. It is up to you, then, to secure more favorable conditions for your loan.

Let's see if we can turn this loan around and reduce our costs.

When you go to your bank and receive loan approval and a rate, tell your banker that you will accept the rate and term but that you want to borrow on a *simple interest, single payment note* that allows for monthly payments.* Many banks will make statements to the effect that they don't make loans like that. That's a lie. They do so all the time. What they really mean is they don't make that type of loan to you. If that's their response, it's time to change banks. You can't afford to do business with them any longer.

It should be manifestly obvious that if your banker approved your loan at X percent, over a specified term, it shouldn't matter what form the loan takes unless there is something they're not telling you. There is. They want to take more of your money for doing nothing other than not informing you of all of your financial options.

An installment loan works for the bank and against the customer for only one reason: The inequity of government supervision allows banks the right to use differing methods of interest computation, which means all things that look equal may not be. This is true in both borrowing and saving (a subject we get to later).

Let me make the point more clear. Surely you would agree that 16.79 APR is 16.79 APR no matter how you look at it. Not so! In our sample loan your original finance charge was $2,920.72. We reduced this to $2,660 by eliminating credit life and disability insurance and the associated finance charge to

---

*Some banks offer installment loans calculated on a simple interest basis. This is an acceptable alternative, provided the true interest is equal to the cost of a simple interest, single payment note that allows for monthly payments.

finance the premium. So far we have reduced your expense by 8.9 percent. Now let's compute the loan on a simple interest, single payment note basis with forty-eight monthly payments. Your monthly payments would be $145.83 ($7,000 divided by forty-eight months) plus a declining monthly interest expense. The computation is as follows:

Month	Balance	Monthly Interest Due	Monthly Payment Amount	Monthly Cash-flow Savings
1	$7,000.00	$97.94	$ 243.77	(42.52)
2	6,854.17	95.90	241.73	(40.48)
3	6,708.34	93.96	239.69	(38.44)
4	6,562.51	91.82	237.65	(36.40)
5	6,416.68	89.78	235.61	(34.36)
6	6,270.85	87.74	233.57	(32.32)
7	6,125.02	85.70	231.53	(30.28)
8	5,979.19	83.66	229.49	(28.24)
9	5,833.36	81.62	227.45	(26.20)
10	5,687.53	79.58	225.41	(24.16)
11	5,541.70	77.54	223.37	(22.12)
12	5,395.87	75.50	221.33	(20.18)
13	5,250.04	73.46	219.29	(18.04)
14	5,104.21	71.42	217.25	(16.00)
15	4,958.38	69.38	215.21	(13.96)
16	4,812.55	67.34	213.17	(11.92)
17	4,666.72	65.30	211.13	(9.88)
18	4,520.89	63.26	209.09	(7.84)
19	4,375.06	61.22	207.05	(5.80)
20	4,229.23	59.18	205.01	(3.76)
21	4,083.40	57.14	202.97	(1.72)
22	3,937.57	55.10	200.93	.32
23	3,791.74	53.06	198.89	2.36
24	3,645.91	51.02	196.85	4.40
25	3,500.08	48.98	194.81	6.44
26	3,354.25	46.94	192.77	8.48

(continued)

Month	Balance	Monthly Interest Due	Monthly Payment Amount	Monthly Cash-flow Savings
27	3,208.42	44.90	190.73	10.52
28	3,062.59	42.86	188.69	12.56
29	2,916.76	40.82	186.65	14.60
30	2,770.93	38.78	184.61	16.64
31	2,625.10	36.74	182.57	18.68
32	2,479.27	34.70	180.53	20.72
33	2,333.44	32.66	178.49	22.76
34	2,187.61	30.62	176.45	24.80
35	2,041.78	28.58	174.41	26.84
36	1,895.95	26.54	172.37	28.88
37	1,750.12	24.50	170.33	30.92
38	1,604.29	22.46	168.29	32.96
39	1,458.46	20.42	166.25	35.00
40	1,312.63	18.38	164.21	37.04
41	1,166.80	16.34	162.17	39.08
42	1,020.97	14.30	160.13	41.12
43	875.14	12.26	158.09	43.16
44	729.31	10.22	156.05	45.20
45	583.48	8.18	154.01	47.24
46	437.65	6.14	151.97	49.28
47	291.82	4.10	149.93	51.32
48	145.99	2.06	147.89	53.36

Total interest paid: $2400.00

How can 16.79 APR not be 16.79 APR? The interest rate is the same in each case. The amount borrowed is the same. The loan's term is the same. The difference is the method of interest computation. This little bit of consumer deception is one of the bank's major income producers.

By simply asking for a different note, you saved $260—a savings of 9.7 percent. Add this to our prior savings and you have reduced your expense by 18.6 percent.

Let's look at the actual dollar savings:

Credit life insurance	$275.87
Disability insurance	413.81
Cost of financing insurance	260.72
Difference between installment and single payment note	260.00

Total savings $1,210.40

Some other factors accrue in this borrowing technique. On the installment basis, your payments were $221.05 throughout the loan's term. On the single-payment note basis, at the same interest rate, your first monthly payment was $243.77, $196.85 the twenty-fourth month, and $147.89 the last month. You not only saved money in total interest expense, you improved your monthly cash flow (10.9 percent in the twenty-fourth month, 22 percent the thirty-sixth month, and 33.1 percent the forty-eighth month).

My example is conservative. Most new cars cost more than our example. In short, your savings will probably grossly exceed the savings shown.

This loan interest saving technique is applicable to any lending situation. The interest rate, term, etc., are immaterial. What's important is that you *demand your financial option of not borrowing on an installment basis!* Do this after the banker has committed to a rate, however, because if you tip your hand before then the banker will simply adjust the rate higher, which in effect will offset your savings.

Don't Get Locked In

Apart from the additional interest expense associated with installment loans, they have the added drawback of locking you in once the loan is signed. The reason for this is the *Rule of 78s,* which is the method the bank uses to accelerate the interest into its profit account.

Without going into technicalities, the Rule of 78s is a banking term based on the fact that approximately 75 percent of an installment loan's interest has been paid to the bank by the halfway point of the loan. Ninety percent of the interest has been paid at the three-quarter mark, etc. This means that if you try to pay the loan off early you will not receive a true reimbursement or rebate. Why? Because you already paid substantial interest before it was actually due.

Let me give you an example.

This is an actual case of a person who took out a forty-eight month installment loan. After making six monthly payments, he decided to pay off the balance. He was amazed at the payoff figure because of what he already had paid into the account. The original loan breakdown was as follows:

Principal	$15,000.00
Credit life insurance	544.50
Disability insurance	816.75
Total financed	16,361.25
Interest	4,581.15
Total	$20,942.40
Monthly payments	$436.30
Payments made during six months	$2,617.80
Payoff figure from bank at end of six months	$13,761.65

The customer wanted to know how the payoff figure could be so high. The payoff figure plus his previously made payments totalled $16,379.45. He only borrowed $15,000 for six months at an APR of 12.68 (a 7 percent add-on rate), and the interest for that period (on a simple interest basis) should have been only $525. He was sure the bank had made an error. Unfortunately the bank hadn't made the error, the customer had. He should never have borrowed money on an installment basis. He should not have bought credit life and disability insurance.

Remember, when you borrow on an installment loan *you are borrowing the interest too!* That's not the case with a simple interest, single payment note. That's why the original balance this customer owed totalled $20,942.40. He didn't realize it, but he borrowed the principal, the money to purchase the credit life insurance, the money to purchase the disability insurance, and the interest in advance. That's why he paid $2,617.80 and still owed $13,761.65! This is how the Rule of 78s works. That's how you get locked in to paying additional interest if you try to pay off an installment loan early.

Let's review and compare the real cost to this customer, and what he should have paid.

Installment loan actual interest cost	$1,379.45
Cost if note had been a single payment, simple interest note	525.00
Difference (loss)	$854.45
Actual net interest rate cost for installment loan (due to early pay-off)	18.36%
Interest rate for simple interest note (as expressed in add-on rate)	7.00%
Difference (loss)	11.35%

Since installment loans are front-end loaded, your net cost is greatly increased should you pay your loan off earlier than term. In this case, had the customer used a single payment, simple interest note, he would have saved a substantial sum, as there is no penalty for paying that note off early. In fact, by choosing the wrong type of loan, this customer paid well over 100 percent of what the loan should have cost in interest.

To sum up, borrowing on installments may cost you thousands you should not have spent, and lock you into a situation where there is a penalty for paying the loan off early.

Never forget this important fact, which most people never fully understand. *Knowing how to borrow is just as important as knowing how and where to invest your savings.*

How Banks Loan the Same Money Time and Time Again

There is another critical question on the subject of installment loans, and that is, what interest rate return does the bank actually make on your loan? Most will say that the bank earns a return equal to the APR listed on the loan document. That's wrong. They make more than that.

To review, when you borrow money on a simple interest note you are only charged the interest rate times the amount owed at any given time. That is to say that when you make a payment your next month's interest is calculated on the principal minus your last month's principal reduction. That's not the case with an installment loan. As explained earlier, installment loan interest is calculated on the original balance times the add-on interest rate throughout the term of the loan. That's the principle of front-end loading. What does this mean to you? It means that the bank is reloaning your monthly payments to other borrowers even though you are still paying interest on the same money.

Let's use an example of $10 million of installment loans.

Assume 50 percent of the borrowers purchase credit life and disability insurance. All loans are for 48 months at a 9.5 percent add-on rate (16.79 APR). The loans look like this:

Amount borrowed	$10,000,000
Insurance premiums	500,000
Total amount borrowed	10,500,000
Interest (48 months at 16.79 APR)	3,990,000
Total owed	$14,490,000
Total monthly payments ($14,490,000 divided by 48)	$301,875

After the first month of the original borrowings the bank has been repaid $301,875. That notwithstanding, they are still earning add-on interest on the full $10,500,000. They now reloan the $301,875—using the same ratios—to others. The new loans look like this:

Amount borrowed	$301,875
Insurance premiums	15,093
Total amount borrowed	$316,968
Interest (48 months at 16.79 APR)	120,447
Total owed	$437,415
Total monthly payments ($437,415 divided by 48)	$9,112

The bank now has another $9,112 to reloan once again. At this point the same money has been partially loaned to many, many different people—all of whom are paying interest on the original balance.

This happens each month. Theoretically, this lending

chain could go on to infinity. In our example the bank loaned $10 million to start with. Each month they have, from the repayments, $301,875 to reloan to others. Then out of the repayments on that money they have another $9,112 to again reloan. And, with each reloaning, the events reoccur 48 times, or during the length of the loan's term.

So, how much does the bank actually earn on money they lend via installments? It's impossible to say. It depends on the aggressiveness of the bank's loan department. Regardless of the actual amount, the point for consumers to remember is, when you borrow money with an installment loan you are letting the bank loan, reloan, and reloan again, money you are still paying for.

Credit Life and Disability Insurance

Previously, I discussed how to effectively reduce your borrowing expense. One aspect of that discussion was to make clear that you shouldn't purchase credit life and disability insurance from a bank, or any lender for that matter. Let me explain why.

Credit life insurance is insurance offered through the lender that will pay the lender the balance of your loan liability should you die. In short, it pays the bank the balance of the loan at the time of your death. Obviously then, what you are purchasing is a rapidly decreasing term policy as most installment loans have terms of forty-eight months or less. Additionally, some policies have exceptions for suicides, death that occurs within a predetermined time after signing the loan, etc. The actual coverage varies with each insurer. Disability insurance is also offered through the lender and guarantees your monthly loan payment will be made should you become disabled and unable to work. Usually, you must buy the credit life insurance before you can buy the disability insurance.

Of course, like most insurance policies, credit life and disability are written in insurancese for the purpose of selling something other than what the consumer believes he or she is buying. And the cost is higher than most borrowers realize!

Let's go back to our sample loan.

Sample Car Loan

16.79 APR for 48 months

Principal	$7,000.00
Credit life insurance	275.87
Disability insurance	413.81
Amount financed	7,689.68
Finance charge	2,920.72
Total due	$10,610.40
Monthly payments	$221.05

Remember, this example is for forty-eight months at 16.79 APR (9.5 percent add-on rate).

The total cost for the credit life and disability insurance is $689.68. That is equal to 9.8 percent of the principal. It represents 6.5 percent of the total loan. That means that you are, in this example, going to make 3.12 payments just for the insurance coverage. If this were a joint loan and you purchased joint coverage the cost would be even higher!

If you check the last section you will see that without the insurance coverage your loan payments are reduced to $201.25. That's a monthly savings of $19.80, or 8.9 percent. You would have reduced your total owed to the bank by $950.40, or 13.6 percent. Best of all, and this is what most people fail to realize and lenders conveniently fail to mention, you have reduced your finance charge! Why? Because the lender makes the insurance premium part of the loan itself and therefore, because you're *borrowing* the premium cost, it is subject to a finance charge.

The cost of the loan insurance in our example is $689.68 ($275.87 plus $413.81). The hidden cost is the difference between the two examples' finance charges, or $260.72 ($2,920.72 less $2,660.00). You won't find that amount on the loan contract. Clearly, this is an example of how the current Truth-in-Lending Law still does not offer the consumer adequate loan disclosure! That added hidden cost represents additional finance charge costs of 9.8 percent. It increases the true cost of the insurance alone by 37.8 percent ($260.72 divided by $689.68).

The real cost of the insurance, then, is $950.40 ($689.68 plus $260.72). You won't find that figure on the loan form either.

Earlier I mentioned that the insurance cost represented 9.8 percent of the principal. With the finance charge that figure jumps to 13.6 percent.

The real crux of the issue is that the customer isn't purchasing what he thinks he is purchasing. Neither credit life nor disability insurance, as used in this context, insures the consumer. They insure the lender. In the case of credit life insurance, if you die the check will be issued and sent to the bank for the sole purpose of paying the bank the loan's remaining balance. It may be more beneficial for your family to take the monies, use them for other needs, and continue to make the monthly payments as agreed. But the money is not theirs to take. It belongs to the bank. All you have done by purchasing credit life insurance is to have relieved the bank from its responsibility of collecting a possible debt problem due to the death of one of their borrowers. Remembering the Rule of 78s, this insurance early pay-off actually increases the bank's net return on your loan. The bank profits in two ways, both at your expense.

That notwithstanding, you should realize that credit life insurance is a bet between you and the insurer (the bank is not the insurer, they are an agent of the insurance company) that you will die before paying off the loan. It is a bad consumer bet, and the bank and the insurance company know it.

In fact, credit life is a major bank moneymaker. Though banks and insurance companies are reluctant to disclose exact figures, it is generally agreed that credit life payouts total less than *3 percent* of the premiums collected. That ought to give you a rough idea of how valuable the policy is to you and your family. Statistically, it's worthless. To the bank, it's a gold-mine.

Disability insurance is another matter. Banks and the insurer know that even though the odds are remote that any payout will be necessary, the chances are better that you will become disabled than they are that you will die during the loan's term. Hence the larger premium for disability insurance. Disability claims are routinely denied, by the way, as there are many policy exceptions.

The Selling Deception

These policies are, in most cases, sold without proper documentation or a chance for the consumer to read and understand what he or she is buying. You spend hundreds of dollars (perhaps thousands, on very large loans) on a policy you have yet to read; because most actual policies are mailed to the purchaser days or weeks after the loan has been signed, the chances are you won't read your policy until it's too late. That delay is planned by the bank and the insurer for that very reason. They don't want you to make an intelligent financial decision, and by withholding vital information, they have accomplished that goal.

For instance, they won't tell you that you can buy the policy outright, thereby avoiding the finance charge. They just include it in the loan form in an effort to drive up your cost.

Lending officers in most banking institutions are taught how to sell credit life and disability insurance. The principal ploy used, and please forgive the sexist nature of the truth, is to "sell the wife." Lending officers are taught to frighten nonworking wives with the thought of having to pay the bills if the husband passes on. Using this tactic, the bank usually has very little trouble making the sale.

An even better technique routinely employed is to ensure that there is no discussion about the policy at all. The lender simply types the insurance information into the loan papers. The first time the customer even sees or hears about the premiums and their cost is at the loan closing, and then they are glossed over. Customers normally accept the added cost for fear that, at this late stage, they could lose the loan if they rock the boat.

Still other customers simply don't understand the loan forms at all. They are the perfect fodder for the bank's insurance abuse.

Often banks will tell you that credit life and disability insurance is required before they can make you a consumer loan. Except in rare cases in certain states, this is a lie and a violation of law. Yet this is a routine practice at many banks. The lender cannot force you to buy its insurance, and if the loan is refused on that basis, you have the makings of a lawsuit, perhaps a class-action suit.

Why are banks anxious to sell you insurance? Why else but profits? Although they won't tell you this, the lender (bank) gets an immediate 40 percent commission from the insurer (insurance company) for making the sale.

When you deal with an insurance agent you know he is making money by your purchase—that is obvious on the face. The relationship between your money, the agent, and the insurance company is understood. However, when we purchase insurance from a bank the relationship is purposely confused and muted. There is a blatant conflict of interest that is hidden from your review!

When we purchase insurance through the bank, the bank is the beneficiary. The borrower pays 100 percent of the premium plus additional finance charges to finance the premium, and the lender pockets 40 percent under the table. In our sample loan, that would mean the bank pocketed $275.87 for doing absolutely nothing for you.

Let's go back to what you actually have purchased. With credit life insurance you have an accelerated decreasing term policy. Term insurance is normally a good buy, but not under these circumstances. In our sample loan the real cost for the policy, taking everything into account, was $950.40. That's 4.3 payments just to cover the cost, which approximates 10 percent of your total monthly payments due. That's quite a bit, yet the "benefits" disappear rapidly.

Bank Credit Life Insurance:

Amount of original coverage	$10,610.40
After 24 months	5,305.20
After 36 months	2,652.60
Cost of coverage	$380.70
	($275.87 + $104.83 finance charge)

If you are determined to purchase a policy, you could purchase a whole life policy for the term of the loan from your local insurance agent. As an example, I called and was quoted a policy for a thirty-five-year-old person, face value of $10,000, for four years at a full cost of $180. Let's look at this from a comparison standpoint.

Life Insurance through Agent

Amount of coverage for full 48 months	$10,000.00
Cost of coverage	$180.00

This gives you a savings of $200.70 ($380.70 less $180). And for half the price, you are covered for the *full amount* of the loan for the *entire term*. Clearly, you can use your own agent for more coverage at less cost. In other words, if something should happen later in the loan's term, let's say at the thirty-six-month mark, your "benefit" from the bank is going to be $2,652.60. Through the insurance agent it will still be $10,000!

Disability insurance is another matter entirely. This type of individual coverage is hard to purchase through an insurance agent because of its prohibitive cost. Yet, many of you probably have some coverage for disability through your employment. Further, should the disability become severe, you have Workman's Compensation and Social Security. For most it is safe to say bank disability insurance is simply buying something you already have.

For those of you who aren't covered elsewhere, bank disability insurance is still a bad buy. Within the policy's requirements (an important point), it will only make payments for that time you are unable to work. Remember, you have to buy credit life before you can purchase disability, so its true cost is hidden or ignored by many. Using that criterion, however, means that in our sample loan, you would have to be totally disabled for a full four and a half months just to break even on the original premium. When was the last time you were disabled for four and a half months?

No matter what the exact figures or conditions are, there's an important principle to remember: When you buy bank credit life and disability insurance, you are locking yourself in. Your family can use the money for only one purpose, repaying the loan. But how can you know what will be a priority in the event of your death or disability?

Summing up: Never buy bank credit life insurance or disability insurance. They are grossly overpriced. They offer less coverage for your family than you could purchase on your own. They insure the lender at your expense. The lender receives a 40 percent hidden payment that comes directly out of your pocket. The real net insurance cost, including the finance charge for the premium, is hidden from your review. If you feel the need of extra security, consider purchasing additional whole life or term life insurance from your local insurance agency.

One final, sobering note: Many financial institutional lenders privately refer to credit life and disability insurance as "our license to steal." Unfortunately, they are absolutely correct.

Mortgage Lending

How It Works, and How It Can Work for You

Almost everyone who owns a home had to borrow money, in the form of a mortgage, to complete the purchase. And almost everyone who contemplates purchasing a home in the future will be faced with the same single option.

When deciding whether or not to buy a home, most families are concerned more with the monthly payments and how they fit into the budget, as opposed to the true total mortgage cost of the home. Unfortunately that limited thinking will result in thousands of dollars needlessly wasted. Very few individuals add up the total monthly repayments to ascertain what the home really costs. The bank uses this oversight to its advantage.

I hope you've begun to realize the value of looking at the

big picture. In the next few sections, I will show you how looking ahead can save you thousands of dollars on your mortgage.

First, we have to have some basic understanding of how much a mortgage actually costs. Mortgages are usually the largest debt a family will incur, and the largest item in the family budget. Unfortunately, most never understand what a home really costs. When the banker quotes a loan rate and the monthly payment amount, the borrower usually figures out whether or not he can afford that monthly expense. If the answer is yes, he goes ahead, but in so doing ignores a more important consideration. He should be concerned with the total to be repaid to the bank over the loan's term.

Given the average cost of a mortgage over the last ten years, it is a general rule of thumb that for every mortgage dollar you borrow you will pay back *$4.25*. That means a $100,000 mortgage is going to cost $425,000! When you signed your mortgage document did you recognize a total due figure? More than likely not. Here again, banks are withholding information, or offering confusing documentation, to the customer's detriment.

Borrowers, if they understood the total mortgage due figure, would think twice about the mortgage interest rate. You would demand rate considerations because you'd realize the total repayment expense the mortgage interest rate was actually costing. But, since that is ignored or downplayed, you say nothing. Borrowing $100,000 is one thing. Owing $425,000 is another! The bank does not want you to put two and two together.

Clearly, when you are talking about a debt as large as your mortgage, it behooves you to negotiate your interest rate. For example, a .5 percentage point interest rate reduction on a $100,000 thirty-year mortgage loan means a savings of approximately $14,000. A 1 percentage point rate reduction would save you twice that. These are just two quick examples to make the point that you must negotiate your loan rate! We review this subject again in Chapter 3.

Let's go back to the mortgage. I want to prove that you can buy a home for *free!*

The first thing you have to do is realize that if you follow the bank's monthly payment schedule, there is nothing I can do to help your situation. For the purpose of this chapter I am going to use a sample loan of $100,000 at 15 percent for twenty-nine years. The original purchase price was $120,000, so obviously the customer put down $20,000, or 16.6 percent. This interest rate was chosen as a fair representation of most market conditions. However, the technique works regardless of the rate.

The sample loan has monthly payments of $1,266.80. The total repayment amount is $440,846.40 ($1,266.80 times twelve months times twenty-nine years).

Realizing that mortgage monthly principal payments are refigured every month on a declining balance, you should be able to see that it will be years before our payments make a dent in the total principal. For example, the first payment in this loan is broken down as follows:

Principal reduction	$16.80
Interest	$1,250.00
Total payment	$1,266.80

The principal reduction is only 1.32 percent of the total monthly payment! With this schedule you can see that you'll be paying the bank virtually forever, which is exactly what the bank wants.

How can we tame this monster? The answer is that you *must* add additional principal payments with each scheduled payment. In my example I will use an additional payment of $50 (a conservative figure—you probably can do better). When you make payments over and above the scheduled payment the entire additional amount goes directly against principal. In this case what effect will this have? The startling answer is that by simply adding $50 per month you will repay that twenty-nine-year loan in twenty years. You will reduce your obligation by nine years, or $136,814.40 ($1,266.80 times twelve months times nine years)! And all it will cost you is $12,000 ($50 times twelve months times twenty years)! Let's look at our savings to this point.

Payments to bank	$304,032.00
Additional payments to bank ($50/mo.)	12,000.00
Total	$316,032.00

While we haven't bought our home for free yet, you'll have to admit we have realized tremendous savings. Let's review them.

Cost using bank amortization	$440,846.40
New total cost using additional payments	316,032.00
Total savings	$124,814.40

This exercise, even to this point, has shown you that you cannot accept the bank's way of doing business. Its way is just too costly.

The point to remember is this: Whenever possible, *pay off principal on your mortgage early* by making extra payments. (The only time this is a bad idea is when investment rates are considerably higher than your mortgage rate.) Every extra dollar can save you three or four down the line. This will mean paying more each month, but the extra payments will go to *you*, not the bank.

Mortgage Term

The length of a mortgage has a dramatic impact on the total cost. It's as important as the interest rate, but few homeowners realize how many options they have. And bankers aren't anxious to tell them.

Review in your mind the scenario that took place when you made your mortgage application. After talking to the loan officer, what did you know when your loan was approved? Well, with any luck, you knew the loan's interest rate, the term, the monthly payment amount, and possibly some other sundry, perhaps unimportant things. Let's get to the point. Did you know all of your term options? Term means the length of the amortization, or how many months or years it will take to pay the loan back. Chances are you knew of only one term option, the standard twenty-nine or thirty years. It's no coincidence that the standard mortgage length means the most money for the bank. But is it best for you? Compare the following examples of a $100,000 loan at 15 percent, and you'll get an idea of how much a shorter loan term can save you.

Example 1

Mortgage balance	$100,000.00
Monthly payment (15% for 29 yrs.)	$1,266.80
Total loan repayment	$440,846.40

Example 2

Mortgage balance	$100,000.00
Monthly payment (15% for 20 yrs.)	$1,316.79
Total loan repayment	$316,029.60

Comparison

Monthly payment 1	$1,266.80
Monthly payment 2	$1,316.79
Difference	$49.99
Monthly difference as percentage	3.90%
Total repayment 1	$440,846.40
Total repayment 2	$316,029.60
Difference	$124,816.80
Savings as a percentage	28.31%

Hold on a minute! You mean that by increasing my monthly mortgage payment by as little as 3.9 percent I can save 28.31 percent of the total I repay the bank? That's right! Did your banker explain all your term possibilities? Did he explain the savings? If he did, congratulations, you have a banker concerned with your financial welfare. If not, and the odds are you fall into this category, congratulations again, because you learned firsthand that your bank is not to be trusted. And that is a valuable lesson.

The principle here is the same as adding additional monthly principal payments. Depending on your circumstances you may wish to opt for one method or the other or a combination of both. No matter how you approach it, you have to tame the "mortgage monster." It cannot be ignored.

Completing the Mortgage

If you were willing to pay the bank those last nine years you should now be willing to "pay yourself" in order to buy your home for free. In short, after the twenty-year mark start making monthly mortgage payments of $1,266.80 to your own investment/savings plan. The difference is that these pay-ments, unlike those made to the bank, will start earning you income, not just a tax deduction. What would your ac-cumulated investment be with monthly payments of $1,266.80 invested into a savings plan that earned 10 percent (which is a rate used as a mid-point representation of most market con-ditions) over the last nine years of your mortgage? The answer is an amazing $220,491.24!

Now don't get confused. If you're making payments to yourself you still have an expenditure and it should be thought of in that light. That is, further comparisons have to take into account all your payments, regardless of whom they were made to. The following chart reflects the change.

Paid by customer to bank and to self	$440,846.40
Balance of savings plan after nine years	220,491.24
Total savings	$220,355.16

Again, we're not doing too badly. By ignoring the bank's amortization schedule and adding as little as $50 per month to your payments you saved $124,814.40. Using that time saved (the last nine years of the mortgage) to your further advantage, and making what was a liability into an asset, you have increased your savings to a whopping $220,355.16. We have saved 49.9 percent of the real cost of your home. The bank's way would pay for your home in twenty-nine years. Our way, you have your home paid for, and a savings balance of $220,355.16!

So far I have showed you a sample mortgage and how to save substantially on its total cost. The next and final step should actually be one of your first steps in the process.

It is imperative when you buy real estate that you take into account all the possibilities, opportunities, and options. You should know the home's total cost, the added principal amount you can pay monthly, the reduction in time that those monies represent, the savings balance you can acquire by making payments to yourself, etc. You should have this information at your disposal before the loan closing. You'll need it for the final piece of the puzzle. According to our sample loan you still have a "balance" of $220,491.24 ($440,846.40 original mortgage less $220,355.16 savings balance). To cover that amount you should buy a grade-A municipal bond from a security house at the time you take out the mortgage. Using a representational buy percentage of 6.5 percent (this rate could be higher or lower) to offset the remaining balance, you will need a bond that will cost $14,331.93 ($220,491.24 times 6.5 percent). At the end of twenty-nine years you will receive $220,491.24 in cash and all of it will be tax free since municipal bonds are exempt from federal income taxes. I am assuming that you can afford to make such a bond purchase. If that's the case, we're finished. You have bought your home for free. At the end of the loan's term, you will have your home free and clear and every dollar back that you paid in. The bank's way, all you would have is your home.

But what if you can't afford a bond purchase? Then you must take out the mortgage for the mortgage amount required plus the bond price. Of course that changes a few figures, but you can do the math required to zero out the bottom line. The results will be the same. Perhaps you would wish to borrow the bond money on a short-term simple interest note. That works, too. Or you could add additional amounts to your monthly additional payments to offset the added bond money. There is no end to the options you can put together. Design your own plan. Use your accountant if necessary. Remember, even if you presently own a home, and therefore cannot institute this plan from its inception phase, you can still use this technique to greatly reduce your remaining mortgage balance. How much you can save (you could save it all if you greatly accelerated your additional monthly payments, etc.) depends on you. The point is, these savings can be realized by everyone, regardless of whether you are buying a home or presently have a long-term mortgage. This example I used is one of many possible plans, but it makes clear the technique and how it can be applied to any mortgage.

The most important thing to remember is that you can buy a home for nothing or you can buy it for, in this case, $440,000. Why didn't your "friendly banker" tell you this, especially in light of the fact that bankers like to pride themselves and their institutions on their financial expertise. Either bankers aren't as smart as they think they are or they are purposely withholding information.

Another Creative Mortgage Technique

We just reviewed the real cost of a home mortgage and how it could be substantially reduced and/or negated entirely. There is an additional technique that you should be aware of, as it offers you a great deal of flexibility in the treatment of your mortgage.

Remember that our objective is to cut the term by approximately one third so we may apply the other savings/investment aspects of our reduction plan. This can be accomplished without added monthly principal payments. How? By greatly accelerating your term in a most unusual manner.

Accelerating the term offers the same result as adding additional monthly principal payments. You accelerate your term by paying a portion of your payment in advance. Let's use a sample loan of $100,000 at 13 percent for thirty years. Your monthly payments would be $1,106.20. The total mortgage repayment after thirty years would be $398,232. We are going to make it easy to diagram and understand this technique by using a two week payment cycle. Instead of making our payment monthly we are going to make one half of our payment every two weeks. In this example, instead of making monthly payments of $1,106.20 we are going to make payments of $553.10 every two weeks. What does this accomplish?

As hard as it is to believe it reduces your mortgage term by eleven years! In real dollars that means a savings of $146,018.40 ($1,106.20 X 12 months X 11 years). Now, add our investment principal with the savings realized and you have a formula for a sizable financial success.

This reduction works because of two factors. First, since a mortgage is an amortized simple interest note you are charged the interest rate times the present outstanding balance, times the term between payments. Obviously, the quicker you make payments the less interest you owe. And the less interest you owe allows more of your payment to be applied to principal. And the quicker you reduce the principal the sooner the loan will be paid off.

There is another important aspect. You are forcing yourself to make additional payments even though you may not have realized it, because there is an imbalance between the payment dates you will use and that of the calendar. In other words, twenty-six biweekly payments is the equal of thirteen monthly payments. The obvious reason is that months aren't exactly four weeks long, so your biweekly schedule accelerates your term by one month a year. This added payment is added to the reduction in interest due to your biweekly prepayments.

Now for those of you that don't believe you can afford the extra month's expense I say that some reduction is better than none. If you wish you may take your yearly expense, in our example $13,274.40 ($1,106.20 X 12 months), divide it by twenty-four and make that payment of $553.10 at the half way of each month. Or, you can take that amount and divide by 52 and make weekly payments of $255.27. In both instances your payments, in total dollars, will be the same as you would have paid anyway, but you will still save thousands. To explain, using the weekly payment schedule, your first weekly payment will save approximately three weeks of interest on the principal reduction amount, the second payment two weeks, and the third week payment one week's interest. This occurs every month. And that interest savings will be applied to your mortgage principal, which reduces your term obligation.

Of course it's easier and more profitable to use the biweekly payment plan, but if that's not feasible it's vital to make a savings with what you can afford. It's important to reiterate, even if you don't raise your monthly expense one dollar there is still money to be saved by accelerating your term.

Because of the impact of a mortgage on the finances of most of us it's logical to make every attempt to control and use that investment. That's why I have reviewed these varying options. Any one of these techniques can help you. The principle expressed in this section can be combined and used in conjunction with the other aspects previously outlined. Or, maybe one year you can use this plan, while later on you can add additional principal payments as your income increases. Don't forget, under most market conditions, for every dollar you borrow you are going to pay back four or more. The reverse is also true. For every dollar you save you are saving four. So don't think a monthly savings of $5, $10, $20, or $50 isn't much, because what you're really talking about is $20, $40, $80, and $200.

Mortgage Options

When dealing with your mortgage, again probably your largest debt, it is important to be aware of the overall financial climate. The days of buying whatever you wanted and letting inflation pay the tab are over, at least for now. Let me elaborate. Fifteen years ago one could find a mortgage around 8 percent. At the same time inflation was between 10 and 12 percent. Obviously you were paying back the loan with cheaper dollars. Additionally, a home is an appreciating asset, which made things all the better in terms of wealth building. You had a built-in winner! You were making money with someone else's money in that you had a profit margin between the loan's cost (a liability) and inflation plus appreciation (an asset). Well, like so many things, financial reality has come full circle. Presently loan rates exceed inflation and home appreciation has flattened. It's time for hardball.

To play the game, you have to be aware of all the opportunities and pitfalls that the new climate has created. In the following pages I'll cover some of the frequently asked questions. Just remember, the rule in getting a mortgage is like any other purchase. Let the buyer beware!

Lump Sum Payments

During my consulting I am quite often asked what to do if you can pay off your mortgage, but have a low interest rate on the remaining balance? Also, many people want to know what to do with a lump-sum payment that isn't quite large enough to pay off the entire balance. These are two different questions that require two different answers.

The question of early pay-off should be debatable only if the current investment savings rates are higher than that of your mortgage. Otherwise the answer is self-evident. Anyone who has a mortgage that's more than ten years old probably has a rate of less than 9 percent. The present rate of interest one can receive on a nontraditional deposit/investment is 10 percent. You should keep your money for investing because that rate is higher, right? Wrong! You are not availing yourself of an important option.

In this example, which is a reflection of many market conditions, you can increase your net gain on an early pay-off, because as it stands, your bank is losing money on your mortgage each and every month. It doesn't actually lose money, rather it loses the opportunity to make more money, which to a bank is the same thing.

At this writing, mortgage rates are 12 percent. That means that the bank has a three-percentage-point "loss" on your mortgage balance.

Let's look at another example loan, assuming a mortgage balance of $30,000 with ten years remaining at 9 percent. You, from an investment standpoint, could make a one-percentage-point profit by investing as opposed to paying off the loan balance. That means that you would have made approximately $3,000 ($30,000 times 1 percent times ten years). That's where most people stop.

Let's not forget that the bank is losing three percentage points on the loan balance. You can make one percentage point; they're losing three percentage points. For the sake of brevity it is safe to say that roughly, for the purpose of figuring interest, the declining principal can be divided in half over the remaining loan term. Our figure now is $15,000 ($30,000 divided by two).

That means the bank is losing $450 per year ($15,000 times 3 percent, or $4,500 over the remaining ten years). At this point you should make a presentation to your bank. The bank won't do it for you, because many loan officers don't understand the business and the others are seldom of any real service. The burden of making a deal almost always falls to the customer.

State that simply paying off the loan as it stands is not acceptable. You want a discounted pay-off. Why? Because you should share in the bank's good fortune if they can have your 9 percent mortgage balance paid off and then can reloan the same money at 12 percent! Consequently, you have to show the bank that they are going to lose $4,500 by retaining the status quo. Does that mean they will accept a pay-off reflecting that amount, that is, $25,500 ($30,000 less $4,500)? Probably not. That's why you want to make an offer to pay off the loan for $26,500. Why the extra $1,000? It gives the bank a cushion if rates turn downward, or it gives it added profit if mortgage rates continue to go up. The bank is suddenly in a win/win position. Banks like that.

Where do we stand? Let's go back to square one. Plan one, simply investing the money and leaving the mortgage, would have earned you $3,000 over the next ten years. Plan two, the pay off discount plan, earns you $3,500 plus another $3,500. Where, you ask, does the extra $3,500 come from? It comes from investing the savings (at 10 percent for this example) for the remaining ten years. Actually, compounding will exceed the $3,500, but I want to compare apples to apples.

If you don't pay off the loan you make $3,000. If you discount the loan and invest the savings you earn $7,000. Discounting loans is going to become more and more important as interest rates climb. By simply using some creative thinking your returns are maximized.

There are many variables in this process, of course. Maybe your bank will discount your loan so your net increase is "only" 70, 80, or 90 percent of my example. That still wouldn't be too bad.

Let's review the other question at the start of this section. What do you do when you can make a large lump-sum payment, but it won't pay off the entire balance? Discounting is not an option here, so we are looking at straight rate consider- ations. You have to compare the savings and lending interest rates at the time of the decision. If the liability rate is higher, you invest there. If the investment/savings rates are higher, you invest there. A word of caution: Once you make a lump sum payment to your mortgage you can't get it back, so make sure the rate differential is substantial. You shouldn't trade liquidity you may need later for a very small rate concession. Because if you have to borrow that money back at some point it will cost you a lot more than you saved. Use common sense and you won't go wrong.

Adjustable Rate Mortgages

Another area to deal with is adjustable rate mortgages (ARMs). In some parts of the country they are called variable rate mortgages. No matter what they are called, *avoid them at all costs!* ARMs are not in your best interest because they are designed solely for the purpose of added bank profits. They protect the bank from free-market forces and you pay the cost.

The traditional mortgage agreement was always a fixed-rate loan. Once you signed the documentation your interest rate was guaranteed to remain the same as long as you de- cided to stay at that residence. Your rate was known and could not change, and although your escrow account might increase with your taxes and the like, the principal and interest re- mained the same. Then came adjustable rate mortgages.

The name indicates exactly what they are. The interest rate is adjustable, and depending on the trigger mechanism the bank uses, your monthly payment amount could change dra- matically numerous times throughout its term. Some of these loans have a cap on them, others don't. Some have a cap on the number of changes allowed, others don't. The terms of these loans are varied, but the effect on your payments is not.

Let's look at an example to show how rate increases could affect the repayment of an ARM with a thirty-year term and a balance of $100,000.

Interest Rate	Payments	Total Repayment
1. 12%	$1,028.62	$370,303.20
2. 13%	$1,106.20	$398,232.00
3. 14%	$1,184.88	$426,556.80
4. 15%	$1,264.45	$455,202.00

The increase in total repayment to the bank in this case, as the interest rate jumps from 12 to 15 percent, is nearly 23 percent more—or $84,898.80! These kinds of increases may mean you lose the house, if the monthly expenditures become too large for the family budget. Why the ARMs? Banks decided, in consort I might add, that keeping the mortgage rates at roughly three percentage points over the inflation rate (the historic industry benchmark) was no longer generating enough income. They then artificially dried up the mortgage market in order to convince the public that they, the banks, needed to be isolated from market forces, such as inflation. They want you to pay continually for their cost of doing business. They also like making a huge income from the safest loan possible, a home mortgage.

But what happens if rates go down? Won't you save money? Possibly. But not at the same rate you stand to lose money. Remember, bankers control interest rates. When rates go up, they go up rapidly. When rates go down, they do so slowly. It is safe to assume that for every dollar you might save with an ARM, you will pay it back and more.

ARMs often mean that the consumer is paying more for

mortgage money than commercial loan customers do, customers who are more often a riskier proposition. The bankers have the best of both worlds. Overcharge the consumer on the safest loan, a home mortgage, and use those exaggerated profits for what amounts to speculation in other lending areas—for example, Third World borrowings.

Bankers lobbied for deregulation under the premise that it would be good for all concerned. They said the customer would benefit in the loan arena by a declining slide in interest rates due to increased competition. But as soon as they got Congressional deregulation approval ARMs went full bore, which then in effect protected the banks from deregulation in the mortgage market. Financially clever, but costly to the consumer.

As a mortgage customer you should never enter into any mortgage agreement unless it is a fixed-rate loan. It may be slightly more costly up front (another banking repackaging gimmick), but it will pay for itself in cost and peace of mind.

Of course, more and more banks are going into ARMs. So what! Never forget there are other avenues for all your lending needs. Do your business elsewhere if you're being financially abused.

One final thought on this subject of ARMs. Banks convinced the public that ARMs are fair because banks shouldn't be locked in to a lower interest rate when rates have escalated. History says otherwise. For decades banks made fixed rate mortgages and profited handsomely all the while, even in times of severe double-digit inflation. ARMs have nothing to do with fairness. Added profits is the bottom line! If fairness in rate was really the issue, banks would offer us increased/sliding savings rates, but in most institutions they don't. If you have a Time Certificate of Deposit for five years at 6 percent, does the bank give you 9 percent if savings rates increase to that level? No, of course not. You can withdraw your money after paying a penalty, but the bank on its own offers the depositor nothing when interest rates increase. As always, the bottom line is more bank profit, and we know who pays for that.

Negative Amortization Mortgages

How far is a bank willing to go? Some banks are now offering mortgage loans that actually allow the bank to take all or part of your equity into their profit centers.

They offer ARMs that have a fixed monthly payment. If the rates go up you still make those same payments. The difference, or deficiency, between what you pay and what you owe is then assessed against a balloon payment (usually due in five years). Confused? That's the idea. Bankers don't ever want you to understand this little beauty. Here's an example to show you what they're up to.

A thirty-year mortgage at 12 percent. Principal balance $100,000. Maximum rate increase three percentage points. Your monthly payments, because of your payment cap, will remain at $1,028.62 regardless of increases in rate.

Assume the home has a value of $120,000 and the customer therefore made a down payment of $20,000. At the end of six months the interest rate jumps to 13 percent. At the end of the first year it increases to 14 percent. At the end of the second year the rate is up to 15 percent. After this three-percentage-point increase, where do you stand when your balloon payment comes due in five years?

At the end of six months payments went up $77.58 per month. You are still paying the same monthly expense, so our deficiency is added back to the principal. At the end of the first year payments go up an additional $78.68. You still make the same payments. At the end of the second year your payments increase another $79.57. You are still paying the same amount.

By the end of the second year you will be running a

monthly deficiency of $235.83. That's $2,829.96 per year! Remember, through all of this, even with a fixed-rate mortgage
vehicle, you would have barely touched the principal.

In this scenario you will actually owe more at the end of
the balloon (five years) than when you took out the loan, and
that's after five years of payments of $1,028.62 per month!
That's right. The bank not only made all that interest income,
but it now in effect owns a large portion of the borrower's
down payment.

Never, in all my years in finance, have I seen such a blatant
example of the heartlessness of banks and bankers. They are
purposefully using knowledge at their disposal to the disadvantage of the consumer. The average customer doesn't stand
a chance of understanding a negative amortization loan, and
the banker knows that. Sure, it's there in fine print, but the
bank knows most people cannot comprehend such a complicated loan document. All the customer wants to know is: What
is the monthly payment, and can we afford it? That uneducated position gives the bank the opening it wants to assault
your finances.

Here again I might mention your additional, nontraditional lending options. There are brokerage houses, certain
government loans/guarantees, private money, etc. There are
numerous possibilities, and now, more than ever, creative
thinking is a necessity.

Reverse Mortgages

There is a new mortgage vehicle available through certain
financial and corporate institutions. It's called the *reverse
mortgage,* and its stated purpose is to enable the elderly, or
certain others, to remain in their homes when they lack the
income to pay for the upkeep cost of a house.

As the name implies, a reverse mortgage is the opposite of

a standard mortgage. In a normal mortgage the lender advances a lump sum at the time you buy the house, which you then pay the seller to transfer title. You then make monthly payments to pay back the principal plus interest to the mortgage holder. In a reverse mortgage the borrower starts receiving a monthly check from the lender until such time that the total which will be owed (the mortgage balance) is reached. Nothing is paid by the borrower until the loan's term is reached, and then it is presumed that the balance plus interest will be paid by the sale of the home.

The borrowing limitations are calculated in a way similar to those of a regular mortgage. It is based on appraised value multiplied by a percentage that will cash out the property at the end of the loan's term. For instance, if you took a 10 percent reverse mortgage on a mortgage-free home worth $125,000, you could receive $5,000 up front and a monthly check of $1,175 for a full five years. At the end of the loan you would owe $100,000. This is just one example, of course. Some reverse mortgages currently have terms as long as fifteen years.

There is also what is called the *open-term* reverse mortgage, which allows the borrower to stay in the home indefinitely (title changes on the death of the owner) while receiving a monthly check determined by the equity balance of the house. The payments for open term are much smaller than a reverse mortgage for a specific term.

This new mortgage vehicle is being heralded by financial institutions, investment counselors, "market experts," and financial magazines and newsletters everywhere. Despite the fanfare, reverse mortgages can be a gigantic rip-off.

A reverse mortgage works in the lender's favor in a way that is seldom, if ever, mentioned by the mortgage holder. Each month you pay interest on interest. The longer the mortgage runs the more interest you pay. For example, on a fixed-term reverse with a fifteen-year term, you will be paying interest in the 180th month on the interest on the money you received in the first month. Actually, you will pay for that first month's disbursement (and its interest) 180 times, the second month's disbursement (and its interest) 179 times, and so on.

Does it pay to refinance your home with a reverse mortgage? Think about it! You pay for as long as thirty years to get out from under the monthly expense (remember, in most cases homeowners paid back $4.25 for every 1 they borrowed), and then you trade it all for a moderate monthly "income" for five years, maybe ten. Even with an inflation factor you will lose money. You are going to pay interest on interest on interest on interest with no end in sight. The saddest part of all, on the fixed-term reverse mortgage, is that you are betting the mortgage holder you'll either die or be financially self-sufficient sometime before the term runs out. That may be a very bad bet to say the least! For five or ten years the added income may help out, but what then? The loan term runs out and you're out on the street with perhaps no cash (the home sale will go to pay off the loan), and your monthly income will be reduced by the amount of the reverse-mortgage payments.

But what about the open-term reverse mortgage? Doesn't that allow for permanent residence until death? Yes, it does, but at a very high cost. In an open-term, you may trade all or most of your appreciation for this privilege. This open-term type mortgage is allowed only on premium homes in excellent condition. Still not convinced it's a bad deal? What happens if you have to leave the home after a few years? You have to pay off the loan, as you and/or your spouse are the only persons who can live in the house. The loan is not assumable. Here is an example. An elderly couple takes out an open-term reverse mortgage that returns $450 a month on $100,000 equity. After three years the husband dies. The wife can't take care of the property and has a difficult time remaining in the house for that reason, or she can't live with the memories, or she becomes an invalid and has to go to a nursing home. To receive a loan on $100,000 the home would have been worth approximately $125,000. Compute a 5 percent inflation rate for thirty-six months for an appreciation of $19,702. The couple would have received $450 times thirty-six months, or $16,200. For that amount the remaining spouse would owe the principal plus interest and the home appreciation that exceeds the amount they actually received!

The longer one stays in the home the less the true cost, of course, but the mortgage holder knows full well that the odds are in his favor; that is, at worst he will receive a good return. At best he will inherit a gold mine!

I have given only a few examples of reverse mortgages. It would be impossible to review them all, as each institution has its own special offerings. As time goes on in the mortgage-market life cycle, even more variances will appear, but the principle of operation will remain the same. The financial institution, whether a bank, corporation, or mortgage company, wants one more pass at your finances.

Reverse mortgages play on the fears of the elderly that they will be forced to give up living on their own. There are alternatives. If you do need help in retaining your home, or perhaps your parents do, consider selling to your children, or buying from your parents. You can help one another and both profit. The parents can live at home without the worry of a reverse mortgage, and the kids can make an investment out of their parent's home. With tax considerations (from an investment/ landlord position) and appreciation, the kids won't do that badly! In fact, it may be the best investment they ever make, both from a personal and business standpoint.

There are also many ways for the elderly to save on upkeep costs. Check with your state agencies, as often there are assistance programs to help with real estate taxes, low- or no-interest loans for needed repairs, assistance for maintenance, assistance for health reasons, etc. Look in the phone book for the state information operator, who will help direct your efforts to the right agency.

There are viable alternatives to the potential housing problem you or your family may be faced with at some point. Just remember, the reverse mortgage, in any form, shouldn't be one of them.

Home Equity Credit Lines

Do the home equity credit lines presently being offered by financial institutions make economic sense for the average family? Probably not.

These lines of credit are nothing more than a repackaging of a second mortgage loan. They are popular now because of the Tax Reform Act of 1986, which phased out the deduction of interest for most consumer borrowing. But since interest paid for debt secured by your principal residence is deductible, banks are now suggesting that you borrow for whatever reason (a car purchase, a vacation, etc.) and secure same with your home. On the face of it that seems to make sense.

But the figures don't add up in your favor.

Although there are exceptions, you should not pledge your home equity unless absolutely necessary, as it is your most liquid asset. If you've pledged your home to buy a car, for instance, that equity won't be available if you need to raise money for a medical emergency. That ace in the hole should not be given away for tax considerations.

Even though you will be able to deduct your loan interest on a home equity loan you may not be saving money. Most new home equity loans have numerous fees attached. There is the application fee, the credit-check fee, the appraisal fee, the closing fee, and others. In many cases, the fee structure alone will exceed the tax benefits accrued. And that's even before you start paying your interest and principal payments. Make sure you've added up all the costs and weighed them against the tax savings before proceeding. Remember (assuming you itemize), you're only going to save 15 or 28 percent of the interest you pay, which may actually add up to very little. Don't pay the bank two dollars in fees and interest for every dollar you won't be paying the government in taxes.

Also, some (though not all) institutions charge their customers more than once for the same transaction; that is, they offer the loan package for a specific borrowing. When that loan is paid, and/or you want to borrow again, they will assess the entire fee schedule again before approving your new application. Obviously that's something you should be aware of and avoid.

One final, sobering thought. If you use your house as collateral, no matter what the loan's true purpose, in case of default, you could be faced with foreclosure on your home. That is an unacceptable risk.

Mortgage Documentation

One of the problems with financial transactions is that there are usually some aspects of the documentation that one or both parties does not understand. In the case of your mortgage, the bank understands everything. For your protection, you should too.

Confusion, or lack of documentation knowledge, is what causes people to rush to read their insurance policy for the first time after their home has burned down. It's what causes a late-night phone call to your insurance agent after you've had a major auto accident. It's too late after the fact! You should know the facts before you need the information, and that's never truer than with your mortgage agreement. Remember, for most people a mortgage represents the single largest investment they'll ever make, and a mistake can be costly.

In a general sense, most mortgages contain approximately similar provisions. Those provisions can be modified, and most are, in some form. The following list contains the items you should be most watchful for, but it is only a starting point.

Let's review the major considerations.

Title Warranty: The lender will almost always pass on to the borrower the title expense bill. Although that's not fair, it's a fact of life. However, make sure you understand that the title search should protect you, too. In many loan closings the borrower never looks at the title search. You must ensure that the title is clear and that you have the right to use the property as you wish—to rent, build on, lease, or whatever your intentions dictate.

Assignment of Rents: This provision allows the mortgage holder to collect income from your property should you default. It is a precursor to actual foreclosure. Make sure this provision takes effect only if you default. Also check at what point the lender claims such rights.

Insurance Covenants: Some lenders require an insurance policy to cover loss of life or the ability of the principal breadwinner to work. The proceeds of the policy go directly to the mortgage holder, so don't think you're insuring your family. They receive only a secondary benefit, as they would with credit life insurance. Some states forbid this type of insurance to be mandatory.

Repair Covenants: The wording of this provision can cause a great deal of difficulty. In some cases it gives the mortgage holder the right to determine whether you are keeping the property in "proper" repair. If he doesn't think you are he can force you to correct his subjective assessment, at great cost to you. Make sure you and you alone determine the maintenance worthiness of your property.

Possession Right: This can be worded in such a way to allow the lender to come into your property before actual foreclosure has taken place. (Avoid this if at all possible.)

Waivers: This is the area where most run into trouble. The lender may present documentation that waives most if not all your legal remedies if there is a default. The mortgage document may have a waiver of your homestead rights, for instance. It is the lender's way to deny you rights and free themselves from legal obligations. The possible waivers are so numerous that they cannot be treated in detail. You should exercise extreme caution if you see the words *waive* or *waiver* on your mortgage agreement. The borrower never receives a benefit by waiving anything. Only the lender profits, and at your expense.

Prepayment Penalties: This is a clause whereby the lender hopes to accrue another absurd mortgage fee if you pay off part or all of your mortgage before its term has expired. The clause may disallow additional monthly principal payments. It may disallow a lump-sum principal payment. It may charge a fee when you sell your home. These fees are usually in the form of a percentage of the mortgage balance. In some states prepayment fees are illegal. *Never sign a loan document that includes a prepayment penalty clause.* It works against your interests; that is, you're working hard to pay the loan off as soon as possible while the prepayment clause will ensure additional fees should you be successful in doing so.

Loan Terms: Review the actual loan terms. The length of the contract, the monthly payments, the interest rate, the APR after the closing costs are added in, etc. Don't rely on the mortgage holder's expertise. Financial institutions make mistakes too. Unless you want to pay for those mistakes, make sure that mortgage document adds up.

Mortgage Transfer: Look closely here. You may be giving the mortgage holder the right to sell your mortgage document to another lender, one you may not wish to do business with. This obviously should be avoided. Transfer of ownership can cause problems, as the lender knows. That's why there's probably a clause in the documentation that says you can't assign your mortgage rights to another.

Acceleration: Extra caution needs to be applied here, as the clause means exactly what it says. The lender can accelerate the mortgage and call the entire amount due. How that is accomplished depends on the loan. The contingencies are what's important. Some lenders are fair, others aren't. When you see the word acceleration—slow down.

Foreclosure: Foreclosure is when the lender applies his rights to take back property when you haven't met your financial obligations as outlined in the mortgage document. Although state laws vary, in most cases the borrower has the right of redemption (normally one year from the foreclosure filing). In addition, most laws protect your equity, and exempt homesteads from unfair foreclosure. States have gradually started to side with the homeowner in foreclosure matters (based on historical lender abuses), so negotiations are possible even after foreclosure has been started in the courts. The important thing is to understand what the steps are if a foreclosure does occur. While no one plans on defaulting, events do happen beyond our control. Preplanning is essential.

Conclusion: Although I am talking about a mortgage document in this chapter, the same cautions could apply to all your financial transactions. Understand what you're signing.

Remember, too, it's not only what is in writing, it's also what's not in writing. That's your responsibility. Which means you have to have some working experience and education regarding basic contracts. And that holds true whether you use a lawyer or not. They make mistakes too!

If you never have a problem regarding a financial dealing you are blessed, because the odds say you will. Only then will you realize that it's too late when the damage has been done.

In the case of a mortgage document, your review and understanding are mandatory. The lender, no matter who he is, has one goal in mind when the lending agreement is prepared: Protecting himself at every turn. Lenders leave nothing to chance. You shouldn't either.

Closing Costs

When you apply for a mortgage loan at most banks you will be assessed an application fee, usually $50 to $75. If your application is acceptable, the bank proceeds with a credit check. Usually $50 to $100. If you pass the credit check, the bank requires an appraisal of the property. Approximately $250. If that meets their standards you need a title search and an attorney and will be charged a few other bank filing charges. Usually these total $1,000 to $1,500. Assuming the bank is still willing to make the loan, you are then presented a points bill of 2 to 4 percent of the amount of the mortgage. On a $100,000 mortgage you are looking at $2,000 to $4,000. In total it's possible to have costs of $5,000 to $6,000 on the average home mortgage—and that's before you make your first payment.

These are fees you have to pay the bank for the *privilege* of borrowing mortgage money that is probably overpriced to start with. Let's dissect each charge:

1. *Application fee:* Banks have us so bullied that they aren't afraid to demand money before they will even make an effort to look at our application. Application fees are an excellent example of the arrogance of modern bankers; application fees should be a cost-of-doing-business expense of the bank.

2. *Credit check fee:* Here too is a fee that should not be borne by the customer. If the bank wants to establish your credit character, they should pay for it. Worse yet, the amount they charge is in excess of what they are charged by the credit bureau(s), so not only are you expected to pay the cost, you are expected to offer the bank a hidden profit.

3. *Appraisal fee:* The appraisal of the property offered as collateral is either done by the bank staff or someone they hire. It's the bank's method of ensuring there is enough collateral equity to protect their position in case of default.

But, like all loan fees, you should think through the hows and whys. The borrower doesn't profit from the appraisal. (They have already offered to buy the property, so it's assumed they know the relative value of the home.) No, like the above fees, this is ordered and used by the bank. The customer has little to gain from the bank's appraisal as it based on the bank's assessment of loan value, as opposed to market value. And yes, this too is your expense.

Worse, once again, the bank makes money on the appraisal. A standard home mortgage appraisal done by a bank employee familiar with the area takes approximately one hour. The profit to the bank is obvious. If they hire an outside appraiser the fee is usually split fifty-fifty.

4. *Title search, attorney, etc.:* All home sales and closings need a title search. That's for your protection and that of the bank. Unfortunately, even though both have need of the service the borrower pays 100 percent of the cost.

If you have an attorney present at the closing, something

I recommend, you should pay his bill. However, you should not have to pay the bank's attorney, as is required by many institutions.

On the subject of handling and filing fees I have strong objection. Like the application fee, this is part of the bank's cost-of-doing-business. Every service-oriented business has costs that they have to bear. Banks are one of the few "service" industries that believes they should make a substantial profit every time one of their staff lifts a finger to help a customer.

5. *Points:* These represent an arbitrary fee assessed by the bank for doing absolutely nothing. They are not satisfied with the high cost of a mortgage and all the fees they have collected; they want more. Points on the average mortgage are $2,000 to $4,000. This is nothing more than additional bank profit.

The litmus test for any service charge is whether it is based on a cost analysis or sliding scale. A cost analysis approach, allowing for a reasonable profit, is fair. A sliding scale is not. Points fail the test because they are assessed on a percentage basis. If a bank charges three points to close a $100,000 mortgage, the cost is $3,000. A $200,000 mortgage costs $6,000. But, and here is the cost analysis, whatever the expense, assuming the bank actually spends $1 on your behalf, it costs the same to put a $100,000 mortgage on the books as it does a $200,000 mortgage. Points aren't a fair assessment of anything to start with. The sliding scale exacerbates the abuse.

Let's take this further to illustrate another important concern. Because of points, and the way they are reported to the borrower, chances are your mortgage Annual Percentage Rate is understated. Points have to be included into the loan's true APR and be reported to the borrower. Points of $3,000 on a $100,000 mortgage at 15 percent for twenty-nine years raises the APR to 15.11 percent.

But even that representation is not accurate. Statistics show that the average home is sold every five-years. If that

$3,000 is applied to the same mortgage over a five-year span the true APR jumps to almost 16 percent. Assuming your mortgage is reflective of the norm, that's an unreported 6.66 percent increase in the true cost of your mortgage. Your bank has done nothing illegal here, nonetheless it's fair to challenge the integrity of a financial institution preparing documentation that they, because of their knowledge, know is more than likely understating your true costs. It also makes clear that present consumer protection laws are inadequate.

Reviewing this in actual dollars makes the point clearer. If your mortgage were to run to term, $3,000 in points costs $103.45 per year ($3,000 divided by 29 years). The same $3,000 costs $600 per year if your home is sold in five years.

Mortgage closing costs are an excellent example of why you must shop your loan needs. We discussed earlier how expensive a home mortgage can be if not aggressively attacked. But, it's not just the loan itself you have to be concerned with. The associated fees alone are worth shopping for as they have a substantial impact on your mortgage expense. You not only have to shop and negotiate your loan rate, you must shop and negotiate your loan fees.

Shop all mortgage lending outlets—including private money, which may negate all but actual expenses. If you do use a banking institution, seek out those in your area that have fair loan fees commensurate with a cost analysis of the service being offered.

Beating the Escrow Rip-Off

When you open a mortgage account at a bank, bankers more than likely will require that you open an escrow account at the same time. The escrow monies, collected monthly along with your mortgage principal and interest payment, will be set aside to pay your real estate taxes and homeowner's insurance premiums when they come due.

The banks' reason for this requirement—at least the one they will acknowledge—is that an escrow account ensures that all the bills on "their" property are paid on time. When clarifying this aspect of the mortgage to the customer the banker will explain that it's in the consumer's best interest not to have to worry about these bills. The bank will take care of them, and all you have to do is add a small amount each and every month to your payment.

Some banks say nothing at all regarding the escrow requirement and just make it part of the mortgage agreement without knowledgeable consent from the borrower. Others are a little more aboveboard and inform the borrower that it's necessary and required for loan approval.

No matter which approach the bank takes in explaining its escrow requirement, it's at best offering a half-truth.

Financial institutions require escrow accounts for two reasons. The first reason is obvious. The second is profits. First, banks want to make certain that "their" (that's in quotes because banks see your property as theirs until your final payment is made) properties are insured against loss. This is their way of guaranteeing their loan investment. They don't want to find out after a disaster that you forgot to pay your insurance bill. That would make their loan collateral useless, which might lead to a loss. Further, they don't want to find out too late that your home is being sold for delinquent taxes, or that the equity is constantly decreasing due to tax liens and accumulated interest liens to the lien holder. If the bank pays the taxes and insurance directly they know these things cannot happen.

At this juncture it doesn't appear that the bank is taking advantage of anyone, does it? But couldn't a bank achieve the same verifiable results by requiring that the customer produce paid tax and insurance bills when they become due? How they are paid should be of little concern to the bank as long as they are paid. There must be more to this escrow matter. There is.

The fact is, the primary reason banks require escrow accounts is because they plan on making large sums of money by investing your escrow balance. They are not satisfied with grossly overpriced closing fees (title expense, appraisal fees, credit check fees), exorbitant mortgage interest rates—they want more! That's where your escrow account comes into play.

The majority of banking institutions pay little or no interest on their escrow accounts, which means you are making them an interest-free loan every year that mortgage is in existence. Banks have a daily investment pool called Fed funds that allows them a special market the public is not privy to. Its interest rate has been as high as 22 percent, so you can see why they want to have as much to invest as possible. And one of the ways they increase their investable funds is to force mortgage customers to make non–interest bearing escrow payments.

To show how this works, let's take a home that has a tax bill of $2,000 and an insurance bill of $450. Your escrow bill is $2,450 over the course of a year, or an additional $204.16 per month. Keeping in mind that a bank has, as a rule of thumb, the use of half the money collected over a year's time, you have made the bank a usable interest-free loan of $1,225. Factoring in a daily investment rate of 10 percent means the bank earned $122.50 Fed fund interest during the year by using your money while paying you nothing. At 22 percent it could have earned $269.50, or $22.46 per month. That may not sound exorbitant to you, but it's clearly not fair. Typically the average mortgage runs thirty years, which means at 10 percent the bank will make, in our example, an additional $3,675 over the loan's term. At 22 percent it will earn $8,085. Although that amount may still strike you as being small, the point is that the bank has no legal or moral right to deprive you of this earning asset. Any income is worth fighting for!

Another aspect of this matter that could cost you money is that the bank anticipates costs, or estimates. Sometimes, in order to further protect their position, they overestimate your escrow payments. Even if they do so by only $10 per month, you will have loaned them another $120 per year. If you don't understand your sometimes confusing escrow statement, the overpayment will escalate year after year. At the end of the first year the bank will have an additional $120 to invest for its own gain. At the end of the second it will have $240, and so on. By the time the mortgage has ended they will have the use of the yearly escrow monies plus another $3,600.

The worst case I have ever seen of this frequent practice involved an elderly Illinois couple. Their son was looking over their important papers and discovered they had $9,600 in their escrow account. This quite unusual balance was due to overpayments and tax abatements. Their escrow account paid no interest. They had had this balance for almost ten years. With their present mortgage balance they could have paid off the loan with the escrow account and still been left with $5,000. No one at their bank ever bothered to explain this to the couple. At an average return to the bank of 13 percent over ten years, the bank made $12,480 of Fed fund interest using the couple's money. The couple, of course, received not one red cent!

The question is, how can we turn this built-in escrow loss into an asset? The answer is direct and uncomplicated. Tell your bank that you will not agree to an escrow account unless it bears fair, current-market interest rates. Further, the account will be under your name and control. You will pay all the bills as they come due and provide the bank with paid copies. You shouldn't mind, assuming a fair interest rate, keeping the account at that bank. That way the bank can periodically review your balance to ensure that you are making deposits large enough to meet your coming tax and insurance obligation.

Even if the rate return was as small as 5.5 percent (and you should do much better either at the bank or through another vehicle) the return in our example over thirty years would be $2,021.25. And this doesn't take into account the extra income you would earn through reinvesting the principal and interest. That's not bad for simply knowing what to demand in terms of service.

If your bank will not allow for an interest-bearing escrow account in your name you may wish to check with the appropriate federal or state banking agency to see if the bank can deny you access to your money. In almost all cases (some states are an exception), the bank's requirement of an escrow account is bank policy, not law. If you find that your bank is breaking the law you may wish to file a contingency-fee class-action law suit, since if they're doing it to you, they're doing it to others.

Lastly, I believe, regardless of the law in your state, if your bank is that greedy with your money, you should find another bank!

Additional Mortgage Options

There was a time not too long ago when a mortgage was a mortgage. It was fixed rate, fixed term, and easy to understand. Those days are gone.

The reason? As reviewed in the section on ARMs, financial institutions don't want long-term loan agreements. They believe they are too risky, considering the market fluctuations over the last decade. Most banks are poorly managed, and don't plan properly. It's much easier to make the consumer pay for the bank's shortcomings; that is, isolate themselves from the market by introducing mortgage rates that are movable and retain the bank's profit margin regardless of events.

Some new mortgage nuances have been introduced by creative sellers. When the market (higher mortgage rates) made selling a property almost impossible, sellers started becoming the mortgage lender in whole or in part.

Then, too, some buyers saw the need for creative thinking, and made offers to purchase contingent on some financial lending participation on the part of the seller.

To make a long story short, the simple mortgage transaction, for a variety of reasons, is a thing of the past. I have no quarrel with that, as one should always explore all the financial options available. However, exercise caution. Remember the importance of your mortgage investment! There is no room for error!

It's critical that you understand all your options. To that end I offer this comparison shopping list. It should help you decipher today's market, and/or see additional options that you may wish to employ when buying or selling property. Remember, statistically, every home in America is sold every five years. Keeping up on your mortgage education is therefore required.

Types of Mortgages

1. *Fixed rate:* Equal monthly payments over fixed term until debt is paid. Ideal for prepaying your mortgage as outlined previously. It may cost a little more up front, but offers stability, financial peace of mind, and long-term planning potential. Highly recommended.

2. *Adjustable rate:* Interest rate changes over the term of the loan. Some agreements have rate caps, some do not. Payments can escalate rapidly, in some cases causing a negative equity position. In other cases, one can lose the property, when just months prior there were no problems. Some newer ARM's are convertible, within X number of years, to a fixed rate. Regardless of the form, you are totally at the whim of the market. All ARM's involve a form of potentially dangerous interest rate speculation. You shouldn't gamble with your home. Not recommended.

3. *Renegotiable loan:* A long-term mortgage that is renegotiated, in terms of interest rate, periodically, usually every couple of years. An exception to my negative feelings about this type of loan would be a case where the initial rate is exceptional and you plan to sell prior to renegotiation. Such a case has great financial merit. The renegotiable loan is a more stable form of the adjustable rate mortgage. Not generally recommended.

4. *Balloon mortgage:* Your monthly payments are on a fixed rate for a portion of the loan's actual term (usually three to five years). Your payments will reflect a long-term amortization, but at the end of the balloon you have to pay the balance due or refinance. That's too risky. At the end of the balloon you may have, depending on the loan's terms, no equity for all your prior payments, and present interest rates may make it necessary that you sell, regardless of your wishes. There are cases where balloons have merit, but those mortgage conditions are rare. Not recommended.

5. *Land contract:* Seller becomes the mortgage holder. Title doesn't transfer until principal is paid in full. The interest rates for land contracts are usually below market, which is a plus. My reservations are based on the fact that, since title doesn't transfer until debt is paid, the buyer has very little protection if there is a problem during the loan's term. The buyer has no land equity until title transfers, which may also be a problem. I have no problem with the principle behind a land contract; in fact I recommend it. However, where most get hurt is having a poorly structured or misunderstood contract. Qualified/marginal recommendation.

6. *Rent with option to buy:* Renter pays fee for option price of X dollars at a time in the future. Ideally rent, or a portion thereof, would go towards the purchase price. This form of purchase may be ideal for those who would not, under normal circumstances, be able to buy a property they desire. At the end of the option there may be financing problems, but that's not the fault of the option principle. Exercise caution, get a fair option price, and you should be satisfied with the results. Recommended.

7. *Equity conversion loan:* Borrower presently owns property and has a need for additional income (this is usually marketed to the elderly). The lender makes payments to the borrower using the property as collateral. Although it can provide cash to the borrower, this loan more often than not is a short-term solution to a long-term problem. At the end of the term the borrower must pay in full or refinance. But the chances of refinance are slim. If the borrower had income that would allow for a standard mortgage, he wouldn't have taken out this type of loan in the first place. The bottom line? A forced sale is the only out. Not recommended.

8. *Graduated payment:* Low monthly payments are gradually raised over the first five or ten years, and then they flatten out during the remaining term. There is usually an adjustable interest rate feature included, which is simply unacceptable. This type of loan, while it's easier to qualify for at application time, can turn into a negative equity position almost immediately. Not recommended.

9. *Assumable:* Buyer takes over the seller's present mortgage (usually below market rate), by paying the difference between the selling price and mortgage balance to the seller in cash or through a seller-second mortgage. Good for the seller, good for the buyer. Many new mortgages will not allow anyone to assume the mortgage. Be alert to this when you sign your mortgage at closing. You will want to retain assumability, as it will help you sell your property should you desire. Highly recommended.

10. *Seller-second:* Seller provides all or part of the purchase price mortgaging through a first or second mortgage. Usually associated with below-market interest rates. As long as the buyer can afford the additional monthly expense, and does not allow himself to get into a "balloon trap," this method of financing can be extremely profitable. Make a mistake though, and you've probably lost the property. Recommended.

11. *Shared appreciation:* Usually involves a below-market rate in exchange for a portion of the property equity when the property is eventually sold. There are many variations of this theme, and this is a haven for those who appreciate creative financing. For instance, a family may decide to help their parents (or the parents the children) purchase a property, or keep the one they have, through this method. In this case the financing has merit. If you're buying in with an independent financer you may have problems. For instance, if the property increases beyond expectations in equity due to inflation, or appreciation, you may end up paying a very steep price to your partner. Some agreements contain a clause whereby the property appreciates X percent or you owe additional monies. Use caution! Marginal recommendation.

12. *Wraparound:* Buyer is able to use the seller's low interest rate on his present mortgage. The seller takes payments from the buyer and forwards mortgage payment to the mortgage holder while keeping the difference for himself. The difference is the amount amortized for the actual mortgage and the amortization amount necessary to complete the purchase. Dangerous legal ramifications can arise. For example, the buyer can lose his equity if the seller defaults to the mortgage holder. Not generally recommended.

13. *Buy down:* This is usually a developer's marketing tool. He subsidizes your monthly payments for a predetermined time, which allows the buyer to buy in on property he otherwise couldn't afford. As long as you know you can pay-the-freight when the subsidy term has expired, and there are no hidden fees for the subsidy, you may find you can make or save money with this one. If you actually need the subsidy, stay away. Qualified recommendation.

Creative financing is the name of the game. It can work for you, it can work against you. If used correctly it can help stop the bank and others from abusing your finances. The key is education, and understanding the actual mortgage agreement.

If the financing fits your needs without exposing the purchase to unacceptable risk, then explore its benefits. However, make a mistake and it will cost you thousands, perhaps tens of thousands, of dollars.

I want my readers to benefit from every aspect of every financial opportunity. This short list mortgage guide will help to do just that.

What Size Mortgage Can You Afford?

On the subject of mortgages, one of the most important issues is determining what size mortgage you can afford. However, most families, when looking for a new home, base virtually all of their decision on whether or not they like the house, neighborhood, etc. Very seldom is enough thought given to the financial end of the transaction. How do you determine if you can afford the home? Based on your income, what size mortgage is safe for your finances? In relationship to the home you're considering, how does that affordable mortgage balance affect your down payment? And, if you have an adjustable-rate mortgage (ARM), can you afford an interest rate increase? As you can see, there are many considerations.

Look at the following chart. The first column is your yearly gross income. (This can be a single income or combination income, whatever is appropriate in your case.) The second column is your yearly salary as a monthly representation. The third column is your yearly gross as a weekly representation. The final column is your affordable mortgage, based on the fact that your mortgage payment should not exceed 25 percent of your monthly gross (80 percent of that payment will be principal and interest, the remaining 20 percent going to taxes and insurance). This formula gives a monthly mortgage payment and then is applied to a thirty-year amortization to determine how much mortgage that monthly payment will buy at a given interest rate (in this case 13 percent is used as an average representation).

DETERMINING YOUR AFFORDABLE MORTGAGE
(13 Percent Fixed Rate—30-Year Amortization)

Yearly Gross Salary	Monthly Gross Salary	Weekly Gross Salary	Recommended Highest Mortgage at Time of Purchase
$ 20,000	$1,666	$ 385	$ 30,000
25,000	2,083	480	37,500
30,000	2,500	577	45,000
35,000	2,917	673	52,500
40,000	3,333	769	60,000
45,000	3,750	865	67,500

DETERMINING YOUR AFFORDABLE MORTGAGE *(Continued)*

Yearly Gross Salary	Monthly Gross Salary	Weekly Gross Salary	Recommended Highest Mortgage at Time of Purchase
50,000	4,166	962	75,000
55,000	4,583	1,058	82,500
60,000	5,000	1,154	90,000
65,000	5,417	1,250	97,500
70,000	5,833	1,346	105,000
75,000	6,250	1,442	112,500
80,000	6,666	1,538	120,000
85,000	7,083	1,635	127,500
90,000	7,500	1,731	135,000
95,000	7,916	1,827	142,500
100,000	8,333	1,923	150,000

Note: To determine higher mortgages add $7,500 to the mortgage balance for every additional $5,000 of yearly gross.

This formula takes into account your financial particulars at the time you make the purchase. Your affordable mortgage could dramatically increase if you get a promotion or new, better-paying job. However, if you lose your job or have huge medical bills for a year or two, the reverse is true. That's why these guidelines must deal with your *present* circumstances in order to be useful. Many bankers or real estate brokers will tell you not to worry; that you'll be able to afford more than my recommendations because your career will provide more and more income. Perhaps that's true. It's also true that taxes will go up, as will insurance, maintenance expenses, and the cost of living. The bottom line on the things-will-get-better-tomorrow approach is they very seldom do. Plan for the future using the facts and figures you have now.

Of course, I hope things get better so your housing expense

as a percentage of your take-home pay will reduce every year. That's when you'll be able to start using the difference for saving and investing purposes. Unfortunately, many families never improve their investment finances because they raise their standard of living with each salary increase, which means they are doing nothing more than retaining the status quo. You need a planned balance for financial success, and one way to accomplish this is to keep your housing expense, probably your largest expenditure, decreasing in relationship to your income. The best way to do that is to not exceed the maximum mortgage you can afford at the time you buy your house.

At some point you may wish to move in order to upgrade your housing, but that's another subject. When that happens you should reapply the affordable mortgage standards for that house. It's all relative.

As I mentioned, this chart is calculated at 13 percent interest. If you want to find your affordable mortgage at different interest rates, adjust 7 percent for every percentage point. If the rate is less than 13 percent your affordable mortgage will increase. If the rate is above 13 percent your affordable mortgage will decrease. Here are two examples to illustrate how this works.

Example 1: You make $40 thousand a year and the present interest rate is 12 percent.

Standard affordable mortgage using the 13% chart $60,000

13% − 12% = 1%. For each 1% in interest, you adjust the affordable mortgage by 7%. $60,000 × 7% = $4,200. Add that amount to $60,000 and your affordable mortgage under these market conditions is $64,200.

Example 2: You make $40 thousand a year and the present interest rate is 15 percent.

Standard affordable mortgage using the 13% chart $60,000

15% − 13% = 2%. 7% × 2 = a 14% adjustment. $60,000 × 14% = $8,400. Subtract that amount from $60,000 and your affordable mortgage under these market conditions is $51,600.

It should be obvious that interest rates are as large a determining factor on your affordable mortgage as your income. Something else should be obvious. As discussed previously, adjustable rate mortgages (ARMs) are deadly to your finances—so deadly that the facts and figures warrant further review.

Question: If you have a 10 percent ARM with a three percentage point upward cap how high can your mortgage expense escalate? Most will say that it can go up 3 percent, but that's a misunderstanding of the mortgage and how it works. Actually, your mortgage can escalate 30 percent! Yes, the rate only goes up three percentage points, but your expense increase is ten times that, because the actual dollar amount of your monthly payment increases by 30 percent. An increase of that magnitude could destroy your ability to repay your mortgage. For instance, a $100,000 thirty-year mortgage at 10 percent has a monthly expense of $877.58. If your ARM increases to 13 percent you now have an expense of $1,106.20. Over a thirty-year span that increase will cost you an additional $82,303.20 in total loan repayment.

Let's look at another example. You're making $60,000 a year, meaning (at 13 percent) you can afford a mortgage of $90,000. Within a few months your ARM goes up to 15 percent. Applying the adjustment technique as outlined, now you can only afford a mortgage of $77,400. Suddenly you're grossly overextended. Now you see why I keep bringing your attention to the necessity of mortgage stability.

You can learn a lot from the mortgage chart. It will give you a good idea of your range when looking for housing. Determine what you can afford, add your down payment monies, and you've defined your market range. Stay at or below your maximum and you shouldn't get hurt. Of course, as explained earlier, I would expect you to apply my other mortgage recommendations to your housing in order to completely negate the expense.

Finding the Best Mortgage

Because a home is most families' biggest investment, they spend a great deal of time locating the property that will best suit their needs. Unfortunately, while finding the right home is important, perhaps more important to your finances is finding the right mortgage. Seldom does that receive the amount of time and effort it deserves. Most talk to just one bank, their bank, or the one institution the real estate agent recommends. That's a costly mistake.

What should you be looking for? Obviously, you should be concerned with the amount of money you are going to spend acquiring the loan, but the real savings are to be gained by lowering your mortgage interest rate. Any reduction is worth fighting for, as outlined previously. Don't forget the impact of a reduction as small as one percentage point. That saving is approximately $27,000. As you can see, we are not talking about insignificant amounts. And these are just the actual dollar savings. If you invested the savings your net return would dramatically increase.

Financial institutions have always known this one simple fact that the average consumer doesn't. Small rate adjustments, when applied to a large volume of money, like a mortgage, return huge sums. The question is, are you going to pay the bank in the form of added interest, or pay yourself in the form of savings? A real effort on your part can save you enough money to send your children to college, or substantially ease your retirement worries.

One of the ways you can shop for the best mortgage is to use a mortgage reporting service. These firms survey a minimum of two major lenders in most market areas every week and then publish which firms are offering mortgage money and on what terms. The cost for the service is approximately $25. Cheap when you consider the savings they may be able to locate. Many real estate agencies use these firms, so if you ask your agent may let you look at their reports for free. The main benefit is, in addition to saving you time, their reports will give you information on financial institutions outside your market that are willing to loan money in your geographical area. This is an acknowledgment that many of the best mortgage deals are available outside of where you and your agent would normally look. If the deal's to your advantage you shouldn't care where the money comes from, just that the price is right. This service is also valuable for those in the process of remortgaging.

Here are a few firms that offer listings on more than one state:

HSH Associates
Ten Mead Ave.
Riverdale, NJ 07457
(201) 831-0550 or (800) 873-2837

Surveys in more than thirty states with contact of approximately 2,000 institutions.

National Mortgage Weekly
P.O. Box 18081
Cleveland, OH 44118
(216) 371-2767

Surveys Detroit, Boston, Columbus, and Cleveland.

Peeke LoanFax, Inc.
101 Chestnut St., Suite 200
Gaithersburg, MD 20877
(301) 840-5752

Surveys Virginia, Maryland, Baltimore, Washington, DC, and
Broward, Dade, and Palm Beach counties in Florida, plus
Miami and Ft. Lauderdale.

Gary Meyers and Associates
20 W. Hubbard St., Suite 500
Chicago, IL 60610
(312) 670-2440

Surveys numerous markets. Call for their listing.

There are other, more local services. Call your bank and
see if they know of firms in your area. Ask your real estate
broker. They may be able to put you in contact with firms
not on my list. Perhaps the best deal can be garnered from
a combination of an outside firm's listing and your own efforts. In my consulting work I am amazed that oftentimes,
when reviewing this subject with a client, I hear something
like this: "But I don't have the time to shop for a mortgage.
We're moving. I have to work. I really don't want to spend
an extra $25 for a report," and on and on. My answer is to
ask, rhetorically, when is the last time you made $25,000 or

$50,000 in a few weeks? Because that's what your efforts can save. Conversely, that's what you stand to lose. A bottom-line perspective makes it clear that mortgage shopping is something you can't afford not to do regardless of any inconvenience.

It's possible that many homeowners are victims of a misunderstanding of numbers and how they work in a lending transaction. One percentage point sounds so harmless. But, as I've shown, when expressed in dollars over the term of a mortgage, it amounts to a great deal. That's why you have to shop, shop, and shop until you find the least expensive, best deal available.

Points Versus Rates

In addition to locating the right home and mortgage lender consumers are now faced with another problem. Which is better, a lower interest rate or lower closing costs?

This has become an issue in the last few years. There are many different types of mortgages now, as we've discussed. The point here is, once you have found the mortgage lender of your choice, you may be offered a mortgage option. For example, on a $100,000 thirty year mortgage:

> **PLAN A:** 9.5 percent with 3 points to close ($3,000).
>
> **PLAN B:** 10 percent with 1.5 points to close ($1,500).

A choice like this can be confusing. My experience indicates that Plan B, because of the obvious, more clearly understood savings, is the option preferred by the majority. That, in most cases, is a mistake.

To determine which is best you have to have a formula to

establish at what point one plan becomes more profitable than the other. Obviously, Plan B saves you up-front costs of $1,500. The question that needs to be asked, but seldom is, is at what point does Plan A's interest rate savings recover Plan B's savings?

First, ask your banker what the monthly payments are on both amortizations: that is, $100,000 for thirty years at 9.5 percent and 10 percent. The answer is:

PLAN A: Monthly payment = $840.86

PLAN B: Monthly payment = $877.58

Difference $36.72

The lower interest rate saves you $36.72 per month. The only remaining calculation is to divide the point savings on Plan B, $1,500, by the monthly savings on Plan A ($1,500 divided by $36.72). The answer is 40.84. This represents the number of months it will take for the lower interest rate savings to recoup the closing cost savings of the higher mortgage rate. In this example, it will take a little over three years (40.84 months divided by 12) to recover the savings you would have lost by taking the lower interest rate. From that point on you are going to save money by having opted for Plan A, the plan that to many would have appeared the most expensive.

And what does understanding this math do for the remaining term of your mortgage? The answer is impressive. A thirty year mortgage runs 360 months. You start saving money after approximately forty-one months. Subtracting that from the amortization means you will save $36.72 for 319 months (360 − 41), which comes to a total of $11,713.68 ($36.72 X 319). This saving is a net figure as you have already, through the first forty-one months, recovered your point loss differential. The math works on any mortgage option where you are offered a choice between a higher interest rate and lower points or a lower interest rate and higher points. To know which is best for you the formula must be completed. Only then will you have the information that will allow you to make the best financial decision.

It should be noted that there are instances where the higher rate and lower points would be the best choice. For example, if you are buying a house you know you will have to sell within two years because of an impending job transfer you'll want the up-front savings because there isn't enough time to recover the loss. However, even though such circumstances are many and varied, for most of us the lower interest rate offers best savings. Again, the only way to know that is to do the math.

I feel obligated to point out that this is one more example of financial institutions making a concerted effort to help the consumer make the wrong choice. Banks have entire departments devoted to packaging and repackaging their services in such a manner as to encourage bad decisions. That's why, on the subject of mortgages, the higher interest rate is associated with the lower closing costs. That's the choice they want you to make. They don't want you to understand the long-term ramifications. They want to be able to advertise to the public and crow to Congress that they offer the consumer financial marketplace competition in the form of wide-ranging options. What they are silent about is they package the services to confuse, deceive, and lead the consumer to the wrong conclusion.

This example should fortify your resolve to understand more regarding your banking relationships. A tongue-in-cheek rule of thumb that contains all too much truth is: If your bank offers you an option that looks appealing you'd better step back, check your wallet, and grab your calculator before signing any papers.

Improving Your Mortgage

Obtaining your optimal mortgage loan is not the end of the mortgage equation. You should always try and improve your position. That brings us to your remortgage option.

Since we live in a time of financial volatility, interest rates fluctuate often and widely, so it makes sense for all homeowners to review their present mortgage as it compares to today's rates. This is one of the reasons I recommend fixed rate mortgages—when interest rates go up, you aren't affected. When they go down, you have the ability to remortgage and lower your expense. You have the best of both worlds while retaining complete control of your mortgage destiny.

Unfortunately, knowing when it's profitable to remortgage is not as obvious as it might sound. If you're applying with your present mortgage holder, you'll find that financial institutions are using remortgaging fees to try to make it so costly to remortgage that the consumer can't afford the expense. For those that do remortgage, the bank wants to make enough in fees to offset the "loss" they experience in the lowering of the customer's mortgage rate. If you're remortgaging with a new institution, you are still faced with substantial closing costs that in many instances can exceed those charged through your present mortgage holder. In either case, you have to understand how to determine if the remortgaging makes sense, and that entails more than just realizing a reduction in the rate itself. You have to ensure that the rate reduction will pay for itself after deducting the added expense of acquiring the lower interest rate.

As a rule of thumb, you should start thinking about remortgaging at any time rates are retreating a minimum of one percentage point below your present mortgage rate. When rates fall below that range, go to your present mortgage holder and ask for your mortgage pay-off balance. Then ask what your new monthly payment would be if you renegotiated your mortgage at the new lower rate (remember, like all loan requests, you want to shop your remortgaging at three financial outlets). For comparison only, have them add your closing costs for the remortgaging into the loan principal before they give you the amount of your new monthly payment. Now subtract the new monthly payment from your old monthly payment and divide the total of your remortgaging closing costs by your answer. This number will tell you how many months it will take for you to break even. Only after those months have passed will you start seeing a profit from the remortgaging. At this point the question of remortgaging is self-evident. Either it pays or it doesn't. For example, if you know it's going to take you three years to recover your costs, but you think you may move before then, remortgaging doesn't make sense.

Let's look at an example. Your present $100,000 mortgage has a balance of $96,502.32. It is a thirty-year amortization, with twenty-two years remaining, at 13.5 percent. The bank will remortgage at 11.5 percent, with closing costs and fees of $2,400.

How long will it take before you make a profit?

Mortgage balance	$96,502.32
Plus remortgaging closing costs	2,400.00
Total	$98,902.32

Present mortgage payment	$1,145.42
New mortgage payment ($98,902.32 at 11.5% with a 22-year amortization)	1,030.93
Difference	$114.49

$2,400 (closing costs and fees) divided by $114.49 (difference between monthly payments) = 20.96 months to recoup your expense. From that point on you will profit from your remortgaging.

Getting a Fair Deal on Credit

The Prime Lending Rate

The banker's definition of the *prime lending rate* is "that interest rate the banks charge their best commercial customers."

All other interest rates are by design connected to prime. If prime is at X percent, mortgages are at X-plus percent, personal installment loans at X-plus-plus percent, and so on. At face value, it would seem logical for the banks to have a baseline for their lending policies and rates. Certainly the country's financial markets have come to accept the banker's premise in terms of prime. The concept of prime has never been challenged. No one questions or attempts to negotiate a loan's interest rate downward as long as that rate has some reasonable relationship to the prime rate. In fact, most of us, including major corporate borrowers, feel we have a bargain if we are allowed to borrow at one or two percentage points above prime.

Financial institutions have, for their own purposes, created the public's misconception of the prime lending rate. That misconception, more than any other, costs the consumer billions of added interest expense each and every year. Exactly what misconception am I talking about?

The misconception that there is such a thing as the prime lending rate! In reality there is no such rate, never has been, and there never will be. It is a concoction of the financial community that allows banks to charge interest rates far in excess of a fair rate that can be justified by cost analysis. Of course, that ignores the moral question of the deception. There the bankers stand guilty as charged.

Bankers, when trying to explain prime, will tell you it's a complicated formula that takes into account the bank's cost of money (interest on deposits), its associated expense (such as salaries), its housing expense, etc. Bankers will go to great lengths to explain that prime is set within a competitive environment with related market forces coming into play. Of course, all of this is nonsense. Let's prove the point.

A bank's cost of money should be different than that of their competition, if interest rates are supposed to be a market reflection. It should be obvious that a bank's cost of money in rural Illinois should be different than that of a major money center bank in New York City, as the cost of acquiring and maintaining an account will vary.

Salary expense (a bank's second largest expense after interest costs) most assuredly will differ. For example, bank employees in New Mexico, on average, make less than those in Los Angeles.

It is even clearer that housing or plant costs vary, as some banks are housed in fifty-story monuments while others rent storefronts in towns where the population is less than five thousand. Even allowing for relativity, the disparity is apparent.

Bankers will mention other factors in the fixing of prime, but these are a few of the major considerations. I mention them to make evident that, assuming there was such a thing as prime (the banker's definition), each bank would have a formula that would provide a different rate than all other banks. Prime might have some parameters, but there would be a variance and in some cases it would be quite large. In an ideal environment, the customer would be able to shop for the best deal.

The banker's "formula" starts to fall apart at the bottom line. That line says that if prime were real in a competitive sense there would be as many different prime lending rates as there are banks. Yet, prime is the same in Boston as it is in Los Angeles, as it is in Miami, as it is in Alaska. This is the same as price-fixing. Financial institutions championed deregulation of the financial or money market under the guise that the free market itself was better able to set interest rates, and that added competition would be beneficial to the consumer. However, prime is set in a completely closed environment. There is no rate competition. There is no consumer benefit.

Bankers realize that as long as they control prime, they control the market. The facade of deregulation, and the associated "consumer benefits," has become so transparent that it is an embarrassment to the financial industry. A monopoly by any other name is still a monopoly.

Interest rates are always artifically high because of prime and the way it is set. Money is always tighter than it should be for the same reason. There is an unspoken conspiracy to deny the consumer his right of financial comparison shopping.

Exactly how does this prime control take place? Very simply, prime is set by a handful of major money center banks, again with no competition, and everyone else follows. Each money center bank has hundreds of correspondent banks

(banks that have a mutual account relationship) that call their money desk each morning to ask what the prime rate is for the day. Then the correspondent bank moves its prime rate according to what rate the money center bank has set. As you can imagine, since most larger banks have inherently higher costs than their community-centered, hometown correspondents, their prime rate will always be higher than what the correspondents' prime should be, based on cost analysis. But they have the same prime rate! Why? Because those community banks stand to make additional profit by using the inflated prime rate of their larger correspondent bank. When you remember that even the money center banks create prime out of thin air, this passing on of the rate becomes even more ludicrous.

Besides the deception of prime, and its added cost to the consumer, there is another consideration. Setting prime in this way violates the interpretive rulings of the Comptroller of the Currency, administrator of national banks. Specifically, Interpretive Ruling 7.800 states, "Charges by banks (a) All charges to customer should be arrived at by each bank on a competitive basis and not on the basis of any agreement, arrangement, undertaking, understanding or discussion with other banks or their officers." No discussion? There are discussions every morning for the sole purpose of establishing a universal prime lending rate!

If this is true, then why hasn't the government stepped in and ended this blatant price-fixing?

The government doesn't act according to its own rules and regulations because the government needs the banks more than it needs the approval of the financial consumer. You see, you can't finance a $200 billion yearly budget shortfall by selling $25 savings bonds. You have to sell million-dollar bond issues. And who has that capability? The banks. The banks have become the conduit from our checking and savings accounts to the federal treasury. Without this banking lifeline the government would have to admit that it is bankrupt and/ or start printing more and more fiat money to pay the national debt—now over $3 trillion.

The government will do nothing to protect the financial consumer. Forget what the law says. Judge their intentions not by words, but by deeds. The government has done nothing to eliminate rate-fixing, and very little to help the average banking customer.

It's not likely that the government's relationship with the banking system will change, so why discuss the fixing of the prime rate? It's important to have the right mind-set about prime itself when you negotiate a loan. I state again, *there is no real prime interest rate.* However, it has representational value, and therefore it is something we, as bank consumers, have to deal with. Prime is important to you only when you realize it's mythical—and unfair.

Negotiate Your Loan Rate

One thing most borrowers fail to understand is that loan rates are negotiable. Every year consumers pay millions more in interest than they should have because they are unaware of this fact.

Unfortunately, in most lending transactions the borrower is at a distinct disadvantage. To some degree this is due to the imbalance in the lender/borrower relationship. After all, getting a loan is often more important to the individual than the cost of losing that individual's business is to the bank. The fact that all aspects of the transaction will take place on the banker's turf further inhibits the customer. A great many features of the loan process are planned by the bank to intimidate customers. Making you wait to see the loan officer is part of the plan. Having confusing loan forms is part of the plan. Offering only one loan vehicle, usually an installment loan, is part of the plan. The bank knows if you're intimidated you won't even consider asking for a loan rate reduction. You'll be so happy just to receive loan approval that you wouldn't dare ask to negotiate your interest rate.

The aim of most loan officers is to make you feel less than worthy. In effect, regardless of how long you have been a valued bank customer, you have to convince the loan officer that you are trustworthy. Never mind your standing in the community. Never mind your work record. Never mind your exemplary credit rating. With planned intimidation, banks help preserve their unfair schedule of loan rates.

Most banks have one rate per type of loan. They charge X percent for prime, X-plus percent for home mortgages, X-plus-plus percent for car loans, etc. The reason for lumping loan rates by category as opposed to the individual's credit-worthiness is that the bank wants to let the good customers pay for the mistakes they make with the bad customers.

Let's review two bank loan customers who are buying the same type of car, with the same price tag. One has been a bank customer for twenty years, has 50 percent down on the car, and needs the loan for only eighteen months. In addition he has a perfect credit rating at the bank and elsewhere. The other customer has been with the bank three months, has 5 percent down, needs the loan for forty-eight months, and has a marginal credit rating. What rate will both these customers be quoted? Regardless of the actual rate, it will be the same in each case. Again, the bank is going to charge the good customer more than he deserves in case the marginal customer defaults. That's the way banks do business.

That is in direct contradiction to the fact that loan interest rates are supposed to be, according to that free market theory that bankers always claim they're following, a direct reflection of the bank's exposure to risk on each request. Therefore, if we are to take the bankers at their word, these customers should have differing interest rates, *substantially* differing rates.

A good bank, one staffed by fair and knowledgeable loan officers, will balance its loan portfolio on a risk basis. The bad banks, those unresponsive to the needs of their communities, will lump their rates by category. You have to avoid the latter at all costs. You cannot afford to pay the bank more interest on each and every loan just so it can absorb loan losses from others.

How can you combat this frontal assault? Obviously you have to shop for banking services. A loan request should be shopped for at a minimum of three financial institutions. That's the least you should do. Ideally you'll also explore other nontraditional avenues, as mentioned throughout the book.

Over and above that you should remember this valuable rule of thumb: Bank at the smallest, or one of the smaller, financial institutions in your market area. The smaller bank needs you, the big bank doesn't. The smaller bank gives you leverage, the big bank doesn't. For instance, a $9,000 car loan at a $20 million bank is the equivalent of a $9 million loan at a $20 billion bank. That added leverage will help your loan rate negotiations. Most big banks have a "do it our way or else" attitude, which is going to cost you money in the form of added loan interest. This works for interest rates on savings as well. Regardless of the bank you choose, you should always negotiate your loan rate.

You have to convince your bank, without being abusive, that you are financially savvy. You know how the system works, and you are not willing to pay extra for the bank's delinquent loan problems. Further, you see yourself as the bank's best possible loan risk, meaning that, based on your credit history and banking relationship, you aren't a risk at all.

And, just like General Motors, you expect to be in the bank's lowest loan rate category.

Of course you can use whatever dialogue fits your style. You'll find this positioning isn't as hard as it first may sound. Actually, it's quite easy once you get the hang of it.

Be warned, however, in bigger banks it may not work, because they don't think they need your business. But if that's the case, and you really do have a good credit rating, you should immediately move all your accounts to a bank that will appreciate them. You don't need or want a free toaster and/or any other trinkets banks give out when one establishes a banking relationship. You want something that means something. You want loan rate considerations!

Financial Statement Preparation

At some point in your life you are going to be asked to prepare a personal financial statement. That statement will then be used as one of, or in some cases the only, determining factor in the approval or rejection of your loan request.

Many banks require a financial statement with all loan applications, secured or unsecured, over a specific dollar amount. A statement is almost always required for loans that are not collateralized.

For nearly all of us, a financial statement has little meaning. We fill it out without much thought other than trying to get it over with as soon as possible. That's a mistake. That financial statement is an integral factor in the success or failure of your application! It is imperative that you understand its importance in the lending process. There is a way to prepare a financial statement that will invariably allow for prudent credit to be approved. Here are some specifics.

The first thing I have to warn you about is your loan officer

and his willingness in assisting you in the statement's preparation. If this offer is made to you, decline. Take the statement
home and prepare it at your discretion. The reason for this
do-it-yourself approach is simple. The loan officer's offer of
help is an attempt to help the bank ensure the legitimacy of
the figures the statement represents. Their ulterior motive is
to stop you from inflating your net worth. That's almost impossible if the loan officer walks you through the form.

Understand, although the bank doesn't want you to enhance your figures, you want to do exactly that! Statement
enhancement is often necessary to receive the fair consideration your request deserves. More on that shortly.

Before proceeding let me give you the Golden Rule of financial statement preparation: *Never lie!* To do so in order to
secure loan approval is against the law and severely punish-
able.

Wait a minute! First I tell you to "enhance" your statement
and then I tell you not to lie. Aren't we talking a conflict here?
No, not really.

Obviously those items on a statement that can be verified
must be presented accurately. This includes items like bank
account balances, stock ownership, and cash-surrender value
of life insurance. These can never be tampered with. In case
of loan default or bankruptcy, one of the first things a bank
does is recheck all submitted documentation, and that includes financial statements. They will verify every entry on
every form in order to try to prove fraud. That increases their
chance of recovery, as it gives them legal leverage. They can
file a civil law suit or press criminal actions against you. Possibly this will allow them a claim on their insurance policy.

Even if the worst does not occur, a bank financial or
regulatory audit may cause you trouble. Examiners and auditors check loan files and that means they review financial
statements. Your odds of getting caught are high. The penal-

ties are stiff. Frankly, it's not only wrong, it's not worth it. Are you confused? Don't be. My point will become clear shortly.

Realizing that all verifiable items are not fair game for our task of net-worth enhancement, we're left with the obvious. A financial statement by design is ripe for abuse. In many cases the bank is asking for our subjective opinion regarding asset worth. This is especially true with your house, personal items, cars, furniture, etc. This is where we'll get the job done.

Look at the following two examples.

The second form presents a completely different, more positive, financial picture than the first. Yet, we didn't lie to the bank. Those items that are verifiable are completely accurate. Those items that are open to subjective interpretation are reported in a manner favorable to the borrower. Let's examine the differences.

1. *Cash on hand and in banks:* I increased this by $3,000. It can always be said that this was cash in our possession at the time we prepared the statement. There is no way this can be proven wrong as long as you use common sense. But don't grossly overstate or you're going to cause yourself unnecessary grief.

2. *Real estate owned:* I increased this by $20,000. This is my subjective opinion of the value of the house. There is no law that says I have to be a real estate appraiser! Again, use some common sense.

3. *Automobiles and personal property:* Here again, the bank asked my opinion. I gave it to them.

4. *Other assets:* This, too, calls for common sense. For this example I increased the value by $7,500.

You will notice that I increased the source of income by $10,000. This may not be appropriate for you, but I want to

PERSONAL FINANCIAL STATEMENT   **FORM I**

IMPORTANT: Read these directions before completing this Statement

☐ If you are applying for individual credit in your own name and are relying on your own income or assets and not the income or assets of another person as the basis for repayment of the credit requested complete only sections 1 and 3

☐ If you are applying for print credit with another person complete all Sections providing information on Section 2 about the joint applicant

☐ If you are applying for individual credit but are relying on income from alimony, child support, or separate maintenance or on the income of assets of another person as a basis for repayment of the credit requested, complete Sections providing information in Section 2 about the person on whose alimony, support, or maintenance payments or income or assets you are relying

☐ If this statement relates to your guaranty of the indebtedness of other person(s), firm(s), or corporation(s) complete Sections 1 and 3

SECTION 1 - INDIVIDUAL INFORMATION (Type or Print)	SECTION 2 - OTHER PARTY INFORMATION (Type or Print)
Name John Smith	Name
Residence Address 112 First St.	Residence Address
City, State & Zip Anywhere, USA	City, State & Zip
Position or Occupation Foreman	Position or Occupation
Business Name Smith's Construction	Business Name
Business Address 222 Jones Ln.	Business Address
City, State & Zip Anywhere, USA	City, State & Zip
Res. Phone 555-3232 Bus. Phone 555-4444	Res. Phone Bus. Phone

SECTION 3 - STATEMENT OR FINANCIAL CONDITION AS OF _____ 19 __

ASSETS (Do not include Assets of doubtful value)	In Dollars (Omit cents)		LIABILITIES	In Dollars (Omit cents)	
Cash on hand and in banks		500	Notes payable to banks - secured	4	500
U.S. Gov't & Marketable Securities - see Schedule A			Notes payable to banks - unsecured		
Non-Marketable Securities - see Schedule B		500	Due to brokers		
Securities held by broker in margin accounts	2	000	Amounts payable to others - secured		
Restricted or control stocks			Amounts payable to others - unsecured		
Partial interest in Real Estate Equities - see Schedule C			Accounts and bills due		
			Unpaid income tax		
Real Estate Owned - see Schedule D	50	000	Other unpaid taxes and interest		
Loans Receivable		500	Real estate mortgages payable		
Automobiles and other personal property	13	000	see Schedule D	27	500
Cash value-life insurance-see Schedule E		900	Other debts - itemize		
Other assets - itemize					
Boat	2	500			
Construction Tools	1	000			
			TOTAL LIABILITIES	32	000
			NET WORTH	38	900
TOTAL ASSETS	70	900	TOTAL LIAB AND NET WORTH	70	900

SOURCES OF INCOME FOR YEAR ENDED _____,19__	PERSONAL INFORMATION
Salary, bonuses & commissions $ 24,000.00	Do you have a will? YES If so, name of executor
Dividends	wife
Real estate income	Are you a partner or officer in any other venture? If so, describe
Other income (Alimony, child support, or separate maintenance	No
income need not be revealed if you do not wish to have it	Are you obligated to pay alimony, child support or separate maintenance payments? If so describe
considered as a basis for repaying this obligation)	No
	Are any assets pledged other than as described on schedules? If so describe
TOTAL $ 24,000.00	No
CONTINGENT LIABILITES	Income tax settled through (date) Current
Do you have any contingent liabilites? If so, describe	Are you a defendant in any suits or legal actions?
None	No
As indorser, co-maker or guarantor? $	Personal bank accounts carried at
On leases or contracts? $	.1st Natl. Bank
Legal claims $	
Other special debt $	Have you ever been declared bankrupt? If so, describe
Amount of contested income tax liens $	No

(COMPLETE SCHEDULES AND SIGN ON REVERSE SIDE)

PERSONAL FINANCIAL STATEMENT   **FORM II**

IMPORTANT: Read these directions before completing this Statement

☐ If you are applying for individual credit in your own name and are relying on your own income or assets and not the income or assets of another person as the basis for repayment of the credit requested complete only sections 1 and 3

☐ If you are applying for print credit with another person complete all Sections providing information on Section 2 about the joint applicant

☐ If you are applying for individual credit but are relying on income from alimony, child support, or separate maintenance or on the income of assets of another person as a basis for repayment of the credit requested, complete Sections providing information in Section 2 about the person on whose alimony, support, or maintenance payments or income or assets you are relying

☐ If this statement relates to your guaranty of the indebtedness of other person(s), firm(s), or corporation(s) complete Sections 1 and 3

SECTION 1 - INDIVIDUAL INFORMATION (Type or Print)	SECTION 2 - OTHER PARTY INFORMATION (Type or Print)
Name John Smith	Name
Residence Address 112 First St.	Residence Address
City, State & Zip Anywhere, USA	City, State & Zip
Position or Occupation Foreman	Position or Occupation
Business Name Smith's Construction	Business Name
Business Address 222 Jones Ln.	Business Address
City, State & Zip Anywhere, USA	City, State & Zip
Res. Phone 555-3232 Bus. Phone 555-4444	Res. Phone Bus. Phone

SECTION 3 - STATEMENT OR FINANCIAL CONDITION AS OF _____ 19 __

ASSETS (Do not include Assets of doubtful value)	In Dollars (Omit cents)		LIABILITIES	In Dollars (Omit cents)	
Cash on hand and in banks	3	500	Notes payable to banks - secured	4	500
U.S. Gov't & Marketable Securities - see Schedule A			Notes payable to banks - unsecured		
Non-Marketable Securities - see Schedule B		500	Due to brokers		
Securities held by broker in margin accounts	2	000	Amounts payable to others - secured		
Restricted or control stocks			Amounts payable to others - unsecured		
Partial interest in Real Estate Equities - see Schedule C			Accounts and bills due		
			Unpaid income tax		
Real Estate Owned - see Schedule D	70	000	Other unpaid taxes and interest		
Loans Receivable		500	Real estate mortgages payable see Schedule D	27	500
Automobiles and other personal property	28	000			
Cash value-life insurance-see Schedule E		900	Other debts - itemize		
Other assets - itemize					
Boat	7	000			
Construction Tools	4	000			
			TOTAL LIABILITIES	32	000
			NET WORTH	84	400
TOTAL ASSETS	116	400	TOTAL LIAB AND NET WORTH	116	400

SOURCES OF INCOME FOR YEAR ENDED _____,19_	PERSONAL INFORMATION
Salary, bonuses & commissions $ 24,000.00	Do you have a will? _YES_ If so, name of executor wife
Dividends	
Real estate income	Are you a partner or officer in any other venture? If so, describe No
Other income (Alimony, child support, or separate maintenance	
income need not be revealed if you do not wish to have it	Are you obligated to pay alimony, child support or separate maintenance payments? If so describe
considered as a basis for repaying this obligation)	No
Anticipated Bonus 10,000.00	
	Are any assets pledged other than as described on schedules? If so describe
TOTAL $ 34,000.00	No
CONTINGENT LIABILITES	
Do you have any contingent liabilites? If so, describe	Income tax settled through (date) _Current_
	Are you a defendant in any suits or legal actions? No
As indorser, co-maker or guarantor? $	Personal bank accounts carried at
On leases or contracts? $	1st Natl. Bank
Legal claims $	
Other special debt $	Have you ever been declared bankrupt? If so, describe
Amount of contested income tax liens $	No

(COMPLETE SCHEDULES AND SIGN ON REVERSE SIDE)

point out all the creative possibilities. This example assumes that your company has some sort of bonus or profit-sharing plan. Assuming that, and making sure that you indicate the money is "anticipated," you may wish to take advantage of increasing your income on the statement. You can't make something like this up, but if there is the slightest chance of additional income, report it!

What have we accomplished through all this? By taking advantage of the leeway in the personal financial statement form, you have become a more desirable loan and general bank customer. It goes hand in hand with creating the image you need to be treated fairly at your bank. It's unfortunate that most banks don't treat their regular customers that well. They reserve prompt loan approval, loan rate concessions, the waiving of service charges, for their more affluent customers. By creating an image with your financial statement, you will be included in this category.

Let's look at what it does to a loan request. For example, assume an unsecured application for $15,000 for four years. Some of the ratios the loan officer will be concerned with are as follows:

Borrowing to net worth:

Form I = 38.56%

Form II = 17.77%

Repayment % of total income for 4 yrs.

Form I = 15.63%

Form II = 11.03%

In each case, the lower the percentage, the better chance of loan approval. The loan becomes more desirable in the lender's eye, because in each case, with Form II, the bank will believe the loan is more secure. These are the same criteria an examiner would use.

Common sense dictates Form II has a better chance of approval than Form I.

Enhancing your statement is more necessary than ever, now that deregulation has allowed banks to branch out into other towns and states. Now your loan approval or denial may come from a home office far removed from your bank. Those people don't know you. They're number crunchers, and the better you make your numbers look the better your chances. The point is, in many cases you can't rely on your personal relationships at the bank to get the job done. The people at your bank or branch may have little to say about your loan approval. Even in community banks, oftentimes all loans are approved by a loan and discount committee. This committee is made up of a few bank officers and a number of bank directors, who may not know you except as a financial statement. This is one of the reasons that "character" in the Five Cs of credit has disappeared. The number crunchers have taken over.

However your bank is set up, you should prepare a financial statement in advance. Make up one now and give it to your banker for your file. Update it every six months whether you use it or not. In this way you will impress your banker both with your numbers and your apparent knowledge of the inner workings of the bank and the loan department. If you have a favorable statement already on file, your banker will treat you with more respect and consideration. That's human nature.

I would never advocate doing anything illegal or immoral. Yet the need to deal with the reality of how banks do business sometimes puts my ethics in conflict. Personal financial statement preparation is one of those subjects where this comes into play. It is unfortunate that enhancing your statement is necessary, but it is. A person should be able to tell the whole truth and receive fair consideration from a bank. My experience shows that's not the case.

There is one thing to remember about the loan approval process. No matter what you put down on your financial statement, the loan officer (the loan and discount committee, board, home office, or whatever), in an attempt to protect the bank, will discount your reflected net worth by a minimum of 20 to 30 percent! That's fact.

I recommend enhancing your statement, not to take advantage of the bank, but rather so you receive credit for what you would legitimately reflect as a net worth. If you don't enhance, the bank's subsequent actions will deflate your true net worth. If you enhance, you will offset the bank's adjustment and be back to square one.

Bank statement discounting is called *low-balling*, and all bank officers are familiar with the term. It is universally practiced on many fronts. It is done with financial statements. It is done with property appraisals. You name it, the bank low-balls it. They do so to further protect their equity positions on loans. The point is, as subjective as you may be when preparing your statement, I can assure you the bank will be equally so in the opposite direction.

Loan officers cannot make too many mistakes and still be employed at their inflated salary level. That is why they feel it is to their advantage to be financially conservative in their loan decisions. This is especially true with personal loans. For some reason, banks trust corporations more than individuals. So with a consumer loan, officers believe there isn't any percentage in approving a loan request that isn't solid gold. They don't like marginal credit, or credit that has an apparent element of risk. One big mistake, or a number of little ones, and the officer will be looking for employment elsewhere. That means we have to set his mind at ease, within the confines of the law and common sense.

Do not forget that some lending is done on a percentage

basis. Unsecured loans, for instance, are a reflection of your net worth times the percentage the bank determines it is willing to lend under those circumstances. Let's say it will loan 30 percent of your net worth unsecured. Knowing that, would you rather present Form I or Form II?

You have to have something going for you in this game. Banks believe they are dealing with a financially uneducated public. In most instances that's true. But, because of their low opinion of bank consumers, it's easier to enhance your financial affluence with credibility. Bankers don't generally expect that a customer knows how to play the game, which makes it easier for us to fight back.

Financial statements carry more weight in the loan decision than I believe they should. But that's the way it is. They are absolutely essential when you are borrowing unsecured money. And when is lending critical? When you don't have collateral, of course.

You are going to need your bankers the most when they are willing to help the least. They are more than willing to help you when you have 100 percent collateral and don't really need the money. On the other hand, when you don't have anything to offer other than your reputation, credit rating, net worth, and other nonliquid assets, you will quickly find out how ruthless your bank can be. That's why you need to plan ahead. Financial statement preparation is one tool at your disposal. If you don't act until you absolutely need the money, it will be too late!

Proper statement preparation can mean an immediate response to lending needs. It can mean the difference between a yes or a no on that important life-or-death loan application. It may mean the difference between going forward with your business or closing the front doors for good. And that's not taking into account the numerous side benefits that can be realized by creating an affluent image with your bank.

A financial statement, business or personal, looks like an innocuous form. Don't let it fool you. It is designed to deny you credit you might otherwise be entitled to. By understanding the form's intent, and the thought process of the loan officer, you can beat the odds. You can be continually successful with your loan needs. Since financial success is usually predicated on having money or being able to obtain it, for those who are not blessed with the former, it pays to know ways to accomplish the latter.

What to Do if Your Bank Refuses Your Loan Request

Before going into the bad news—that your loan application has been turned down—we should review certain specifics that will assist you in receiving a positive response to your loan requests.

Assuming your loan is viable, there is no reason for your banker to turn you down. However, as previously noted, the bank wants you on the defensive. It will help your application if you do some homework in preparation for your loan presentation. This is where many go wrong. They go into the bank with nothing but themselves, a few figures trusted to memory, and some high hopes. That's a mistake. Consistent borrowing success depends on planning. If you have a personal loan request, make sure you have an updated financial statement with you. Have your figures on the exact cost of the car (or whatever) and know your ratios (what percentage you have down, etc.). If you have a business loan request, you should have a complete package, both business and personal. A large portion of loan denials could be avoided if the customer took the time to come to the interview prepared, which would not only help with loan approval, it would also aid in lowering your loan rate. If you can substantiate why *your* loan request is better than others in the same category, your banker will have to be more receptive when you politely demand an interest rate reduction. A complete, well-documented loan application is an invaluable tool in ensuring you receive positive loan consideration.

If your loan is denied, you have two choices: You can try another bank, or pursue the matter further with your bank. If you have a positive history with the bank, you should proceed with the original application. You shouldn't throw away a long-standing banking relationship because of one negative experience. The first thing to do is approach the loan officer who made the decision and ask why he or she turned you down. You want an in-depth answer, not the simplistic one offered on your credit denial notice. Then ask what it would take to elicit a positive response. Many times a loan officer will turn down a request for no substantive reason. Yet, when asked for additional help, they will take the time and make the extra effort they should have made in the first place. Unfortunately, most loan officers look at an application and try to find reasons to turn it down. The best loan officers look at even the most difficult applications and try and find ways to approve the loan, but the chances of finding a skilled loan officer are remote, so you have to be prepared to deal with the majority.

Most loan applicants don't follow-up a loan denial because they're embarrassed, angry, or they think that once the bank officer has spoken, that's the end of it. Not true. If the officer won't help, follow the lending department's chain of command all the way to the board of directors, if necessary. Along the way you may find your previously rejected loan request receives an approval, since for all but the worst applications, credit approval is subjective. All you have to do is find the person who sees things your way. Over and above that, you may wish to consider other actions outside the bank proper (a subject reviewed throughout this book). Here, too, when the banker realizes that you are serious enough to take advantage of your regulatory and legal options, you may find that your loan denial is magically turned into an approval. The bank knows that it is, in many instances, less expensive to take a chance on your loan request than it is to spend time, money, and effort in response to your complaints and/or legal maneuvering.

Depositors loan the bank more money each day than the bank loans to its customers, so it should follow that the relationship flows fairly in both directions—a very simple truth that is conveniently ignored by many loan officers. To combat the possibility of the loan officer's unfavorable mind-set, remember to come to the loan interview prepared with documentation and a positive attitude. If your original request is denied, don't be afraid to pursue the matter further within the bank. If you're still unsuccessful you have regulatory and legal options that are simple and direct. The agencies themselves may be of little assistance, but your continued pursuit of the issue may force the matter to your advantage.

Once you know how to reverse a loan rejection you will always be able to borrow for any worthwhile reason.

Credit Pitfalls and Ways to Avoid Them

The Credit Card Treadmill

If interest rates were relatively inexpensive, what would you do if your mortgage was approved, but at 19 percent? Or your car loan at 22 percent? In both examples you would immediately withdraw your application and move all your banking business to another institution. You would not allow your finances to be assaulted.

And yet, through the miracle of questionable packaging, much of the daily borrowing in this country is accomplished at exceptionally high rates that completely ignore the influence of the market. Banks realized years ago that their non-competitive hold on interest rates could be further enhanced if they could hide the true cost of money from the borrower. Hence was born plastic money, or credit cards.

A sobering fact: Affluent people did not get that way by paying more for things than necessary. That's why you should never borrow for depreciating, nonessential assets. It follows, then, that while they may use a credit card for convenience, affluent people never let interest charges accrue, as that would be adding to the real cost of the purchase. The only people who borrow using credit cards are people who either do not understand the system or have no other method to purchase the use of funds.

Even at a superficial look, it should be obvious that using a credit card is dangerous. That is why banks have spent millions in advertising, marketing, and promotion to obliterate the true cost of using their credit cards. That is why most people cannot tell you what interest rate their card charges and/or what method of interest computation is used by the bank. As sad as that is, it's true. Banks have been most successful at hiding important facts from the credit card consumer. For example, you will often see or receive ads for credit cards with no obvious mention of the interest rate. If your application is subsequently approved you will receive a notice of rate along with reams of other materials, but at this point, after the passage of a number of weeks, most people don't bother reading all the fine print, or they just don't understand. In addition, hardly anyone understands how his interest is calculated.

In any market, banks cannot justify by cost analysis their exorbitant interest rates on credit cards. The proof of that statement lies in recent history. A number of years ago home mortgages were at 16 percent. Prime was at 20 percent. Consumer loans at 18 percent. Commercial loans at prime plus three to four percentage points. Credit cards were at 18 to 22 percent. A few years later mortgages dropped to 9 percent. Prime was at 7.5 percent. Consumer loans were reduced to 9 percent. Commercial loans were at straight prime. All rates dropped almost by half, yet credit cards were still charging 18 to 22 percent. Something's wrong!

The question is, why didn't credit card rates drop, too? The answer is simple. Banks don't have to get into rate competition with their credit cards because the consumer doesn't know what the rates really are in the first place. Also, only people who can afford it the least use credit cards for anything other than convenience, so banks know they have a captive, probably financially uneducated, market. Because of that they don't fear financial retribution; that is, loss of accounts. Can you imagine a bank telling General Motors, at a time when prime is 7.5 percent, that it has to pay 22 percent to borrow money! GM would take its business elsewhere. Unfortunately, credit card users aren't that discerning. That perpetuates their high cost of money, which subsequently helps keep them among the less affluent. It is a cycle, in part orchestrated by the banking community.

Not only are most people unaware of their interest rate, but the system is designed to further muddle the transaction until the consumer completely forgets he is entering into a financial lending transaction. If, every time you wanted to borrow money using your credit card, you had to go into the bank and sign a separate loan agreement indicating an interest rate of 22 percent, you might rethink the purchase. But with a card it's easy to forget the real issue, which is this: Regardless of what you are purchasing, you are in the process of borrowing money. How much it will cost you depends on the card's interest rate and the bank's method of interest computation, but it will be plenty!

I hope by using the following example/quiz I can convince you never to use that credit card for a loan again, except possibly in an emergency.

Let's assume a credit card debt of $4,500 (average for many families), additional monthly purchases of $50, and a minimum repayment of $125 per month at 22 percent. The question is: How long will it take this family to pay off its credit card debt?

The answer? The debt will never be paid off!

With the minimum payment of $125, only $42.50 is principal (the interest is $82.50 per month). This principal reduction will be offset by the additional monthly purchases. This family will constantly be going financially backwards.

How costly is this method of borrowing over the course of one's life? To make the point, let's assume these two people are twenty-five years old when they acquire this credit card debt balance. At the age of sixty-five they will have paid back $60,000 and they still will have a balance due of $4,500 plus. In effect, they will not have reduced their original debt at all. Forty years of payments and they still owe the same amount of money as when they started. We are talking economic self-destruction here. This should make it clear that banks package their credit card "service" to rape the financial future of many unfortunate families. You can't let this happen.

If you have to borrow it should be obvious that you could do so at a substantially reduced rate, as the credit card interest rate of 22 percent leaves a great deal of room for reduction in expense. Almost any personal loan would save considerable money. At any rate, borrowing using a card is not a viable alternative.

Now before you say that you don't borrow using plastic, I have to ask. Have you ever been assessed an interest charge on your card? Remember, some cards now charge from the moment you use the card, which automatically means you will accrue interest charges even if you pay the entire balance when you receive the bill. If that's the case, you "borrowed" using plastic! Others who don't pay off the entire bill obviously borrow using plastic. Remember, just because you bought a new suit as opposed to receiving cash, you still borrowed money.

Sadly, many people will have credit card debt the rest of their lives. It is truly a bank-designed treadmill. The question

I have to ask is: Why would anyone allow himself and his family to be abused in this manner? This is a prime example of paying more for something than necessary. If you have to borrow money, OK. If you use a credit card to accomplish that goal, you are making a financial mistake that rates a 10 on the 1-to-10 mistake meter.

The Variable Rate Credit Card

Above, we discussed the credit card treadmill, and how the issuing companies/banks have designed the system to ensure their maximum return, never-ending consumer debt, and confusion in "creditese," which allows for taking the most from those who can afford it the least. Credit card companies have made consumer abuse an art form, and they have done so not by providing a legitimate consumer service, but rather by exploiting a segment of the financial market. They then expand that abuse further by misdirecting that market segment. A good example is the variable rate credit card.

A major bank credit card company announced to its members that it was offering a variable interest rate on its cards. Present members were sent certificates indicating the option of changing from the fixed rate. New members, I assume, are offered both options, that is, fixed and variable. The variable interest rate is "at the prime rate, as published in the *Wall Street Journal,* plus 9.4 percent." The change, should you opt for the variable rate, is not reversible—once your fixed rate is gone, it's gone for good!

Before going into specifics, let me give you some quotes from their ad. You decide if they're being fair.

"Interest rates have been making front-page news quite regularly these past few months. And, at (name of card), we're committed to helping our valued Cardmembers take advantage of favorable rates."

"This variable rate could save you a significant amount of money."

"For example, the prime rate on June 15, 1987, was published at 8.25 percent. That means your variable rate for billing statements dated July 1987 would be 8.25 percent plus 9.4 percent—only 17.65 percent!"

As their fixed rate is 19.8 percent, the savings we are talking about even then was only 2.15 percent. With a balance of $5,000, which I certainly hope you don't have, your savings would have only amounted to $8.95 per month. Hardly seems like much of a bargain does it? That's because it's not.

Of course the ad doesn't mention the other side of the coin. What happens if prime goes up? You guessed it, your "savings" will be history, and you will be locked in to a roller-coaster ride on the interest-rate express. Historically, we know how high prime can go, and with this variable interest rate credit card there is no cap on the upside!

Of course the timing on this company's market repackaging (August 1987) is highly suspect. Prime was as low as it had been in decades, which made the sales pitch sound financially profitable to credit card users who might not take into account the long-term consequences. Also, the ad only gave examples of savings. There was no balance to the presentation. Lastly, the company knew exactly what it was doing; that is, setting up its financially uneducated cardholders for added expense. Otherwise, why the nonreversal clause, which prohibits going back to the fixed rate?

As of this writing other credit card firms are starting to offer the variable rate option. More will follow.

If you remembered my comments on the variable rate mortgage, you knew up front what my reaction to the variable rate credit card was going to be. Well, you were right, but let's go further. This is much worse than the variable rate mortgage (certainly not in volume and exposure, but rather in principle), as credit card borrowing is financially unacceptable on its face! This new credit card twist is a disgrace. No one in his right mind would opt for this method of interest computation, and the company knows that. This leaves us with the not surprising conclusion that this corporation is making every attempt possible to take as much from their less fortunate clients as possible under very relaxed consumer-protection laws.

You have been warned. Do not accept a variable rate credit card. Of course, if you really want to save money, don't borrow using plastic at all.

The Economics of Starting and Maintaining Your Own Business

One of the best ways to stop the financial industry, in this case your bank, from abusing your finances is never to approach them for a loan for your own business. If there is any time that you are particularly vulnerable to the greed of your bank, it is when you start your own business, or need additional lending. A small business request is a signal to the banker that they can make an exceptionally safe loan with a disproportionate interest rate return. For the consumer there must be a better way. There is.

This book is dedicated to the individual, and therefore not devoted to business consultation per se. But many people use personal assets as collateral for small business loans, so many of the principles of personal banking apply.

Many people today are fed up with the standard career path. You know, the nine-to-five job for the rest of your life with little or no substantial financial reward. The old saying "You'll never get rich working for someone else" motivates many to pursue their own goals. For some this means starting one's own small business. In most cases the parties have little or no start-up capital, so they approach their local bank. The bank, if it approves the loan, more often than not will demand that the borrower pledge personal collateral, such as home mortgage equity, to secure the loan.

Here is a sobering fact of financial life: The overwhelming majority of small businesses go broke within the first twenty-four months. I don't say that to inhibit your aggressiveness, but rather to lead you to this orderly progression. If you borrow for business purposes and pledge personal assets to secure the loan, and if that business files bankruptcy, you are going to lose both your business and personal equities. This happens to hundreds, perhaps thousands, of people every day.

In some cases the borrower will not pledge a specific personal asset, but will sign a personal guarantee to additionally secure the loan. This, too, obligates the signer to pay the bank back with personal assets should the business be unable to meet its obligations. People either don't realize what they're doing when they sign up, or they think "it can't happen to them."

There is something wrong with the course of events in this scenario. Why, if the business is collateralizing the loan, does the bank want your personal guarantee, or home mortgage equity too? The answer is painfully obvious. The bank knows the odds are that you are going to fail. It wants to be secure when that happens. The problem with the bank's approach is that it charges the highest interest rates for this type of loan, and yet it is overly secured with business and personal assets. The loan should be either secured only with business assets at a fairly high, yet competitive, interest rate, or secured with business and personal assets at a very low interest rate. The bank, as it is so wont to do, takes the best from both sides of the equation.

Further, if the bank truly believes you're going to fail, it shouldn't help you commit financial suicide! But, because of the profits this type of loan generates, it is more than willing to become your business "partner." Since it forces you to collateralize your business loan with personal assets it can't lose, no matter what happens. The same isn't true for you and your family.

I want my readers to know that they should *never* mix their business and personal finances. To do so is almost assured financial destruction. This includes taking out personal loans and using the proceeds for business purposes.

So how then does someone go out on his own?

If you had been following some sort of savings plan during your life this probably would not be a problem, but that's another subject. It should be noted that if you start a new venture with cash your chances of success are far greater, since you will have no monthly loan payments to make. Most businesses fail due to undercapitalization. Now add to that a substantial monthly debt structure and you have a blueprint for a self-fulfilling prophecy of business failure. Not borrowing at the bank will help your cash-flow position, and therefore substantially increase your chances of remaining open. A new business needs time to succeed. Yet, with the bank debt structure most use to obtain their business, they have no time. Thirty days after you open your doors your first payment is due. Actually, in some cases that first payment is due before you open the doors; for example, it takes time to ready a retail shop for the customer.

Assume a worst-case scenario. You do not have the money to start a business. Where could the money come from? There are numerous answers to that question. Obviously I cannot mention them all. No matter what you decide to do, the key is acquiring the money without having monthly payments!

First of all I recommend the private sector. What form that

borrowing would take I leave to you. The point is, I want to draw your attention once again to the opportunity of borrowing from individual investors. You don't have to use a bank! If you have money to invest I also draw your attention to the opportunities of this type of investment/lending. Both sides can win consistently. The importance of private money, and of course you have to use prudent caution, is that the terms can be extremely flexible. The more creative you are, the better. This is not true with a bank, where it's either your banker's way or not at all. There is a real gold mine here that demands exploration by those looking for financing.

Where can you locate private money? Ask your broker if you have one. They usually know what private money is available. Ask other small-business people, as they may have their own outlets. One very simple productive method is to put an ad in the paper or appropriate trade journal. Private money *is* available, if you make any kind of reasonable effort.

Here is another viable possibility: a limited partnership. For those who are not aware, a limited partnership has all the ramifications of a partnership, except the exposure to loss of the investor(s) is limited to the dollar amount of their investment. Limited partnerships, assuming they have competitive rates and terms, are usually sold immediately, since they are excellent investment vehicles.

From the side of the business owner, depending on how you structure the limited partnership, your partners will be due no monthly payments, will have no voice in how you operate your company, and have no claim on your personal assets. Are there other benefits? Yes.

In most cases a limited partnership will allow you to raise far more capital than the bank would ever allow you in a loan. Regarding the cost of capital, it may actually be less expensive than what banks will charge. Also, because you have not pledged your home or other personal equities, you still have resources available for other purposes (such as borrowing for medical emergencies, etc.) in a crisis.

You have found the best of all possibilities. Most of all you haven't commingled business and personal assets. How important is that? Let's use an example, farfetched as you may find it, to make the point. The next time you go into the bank to make a deposit ask the bank president to give you a personal, written guarantee for the amount you have deposited. Ask him to pledge his home and his car to secure those deposits. Obviously bank officers don't guarantee personally the deposits of their customers, but that's what they ask their business loan customers to do all the time. The banker won't comply for the same reason you shouldn't. The risk of intermixing personal and business funds is far too great to be acceptable.

This problem should be moot for most readers, as there are too many other avenues available to be a victim of the bank's limited lending options. Remember this, however. Because of the importance of a lending document or of a limited partnership agreement, I strongly recommend that you avail yourself of an attorney for consultation and document review (the fee should be minimal). A mistake would be too costly. You need a professional.

How you finance a business is critical to the success of your venture. It can also be critical to the success of your personal finances. Traditional bank lending is simply outmoded and unacceptable. Creative financing offers unlimited potential with limited risks. Although some of this chapter's information may seem outside the parameters of the book's intent, it shouldn't. In each case where I find fault with the banking system, I feel obligated to offer an alternative or a direction that will help you insulate you, your family, and perhaps your business from your local banker.

In the arena of small-business lending, you are at extreme

risk when you deal with your bank. It is not the answer to the problem. In fact, the bank will substantially increase your odds of failure.

How to Prepare a Small Business Loan Proposal

The previous section notwithstanding, I know a number of readers will opt to approach their bank with their small business loan requests. Others living in small or rural communities may have little choice. If either is the case you must understand the proper way to accomplish this task. As I explained in "What to Do If Your Bank Refuses Your Loan Request," preparation is the key.

This can be difficult as small businesses don't have the luxury of employing a large staff, accountants, and lawyers to do the work. Typically the owner has to prepare the documentation and make the presentation. Unfortunately, since most are not educated in the art of loan proposal preparation, they are not nearly as successful as they could be. My experience indicates that, due to the subjectivity of loan approval, a larger percentage of small business loan requests that are turned down could have been approved with a more professional presentation. Further, even those that were approved could have substantially reduced their loan rate with a better application. The importance of loan proposal preparation cannot be overstated.

But before getting to the loan proposal I want to explain a helpful pre-test. In trying to give you the optimum positioning for your application, the best place to start is to determine if your loan request has a reasonable chance of being successful.

This test represents not how a loan should be reviewed, but

rather how banks do business. A total score of 80 or better and your chances are good. 79 to 65, your chances are fair; 64 to 55, your chances are poor; below 55, you're probably wasting your time.

1. **How Are the Funds Going to Be Used?**
   Business expansion 10
   Operating capital 5
   Starting your business 0
2. **How Good Is Your Credit Rating?**
   Excellent 10
   Fair 5
   Poor 0
3. **What Is the Trend for Your Business?**
   Historically strong 10
   Steady 5
   Unpredictable 0
4. **What Is the Status of Your Business Plan?**
   Written/immediately available 10
   Informal 5
   Unavailable 0
5. **Financial and Accounting Controls?**
   Yes 10
   Some 5
   Few 0
6. **Business Insurance?**
   Above average coverage 10
   Average 5
   Below average 0
7. **Staff Quality**
   Excellent 10
   Average 5
   Below average 0
8. **How Do Your Operational Ratios Compare to Others in Your Industry?**

Excellent 10
Average 5
Below average 0
9. How Does Your Net Profit Compare to Others in Your Industry?
Excellent 10
Average 5
Below average 0
10. How Long Could Your Business Survive Without You?
Forever 10
For a while 5
It couldn't 0

Take the test. Be honest. It's much easier to take my test now, when there's no pressure, than take the bank's test later, when your business may hang in the balance.

Assuming you have determined your application is viable, it's time to turn to the mechanics of the proposal.

A good loan proposal consists of eight specific points you must include and explain. They are as follows:

1. *Summary:* Give the name and address of your business. Include your name, title, and phone. Briefly explain the nature of your business, the exact amount of the monies sought (don't under- or overestimate), the purpose of the loan, and the method and source of loan repayment.

2. *Loan purpose:* Explain in great detail the exact use of the loan proceeds. Don't generalize by using terms like working capital, etc., as that only heightens the concern of most loan officers. The bank wants to know specifics.

3. *Business profile:* Even if your banker knows you and your business well it is important to give details of your company's structure. For example, the company's age, number of employees, legal status, etc. Assume you are explaining your business to someone that has little knowledge of its workings as, even if the loan officer does, chances are members of the Loan and Discount Committee that will approve or reject your loan don't.

4. *Financial statements:* Offer balance and profit and loss statements for the last three years. While bankers are much happier with audited statements, most small businesses can't afford the expense. That notwithstanding, have the statements reviewed by your accountant and notated as such. It's imperative that commentary explaining anything out of the ordinary is included. Don't think you can explain it verbally and solve the problem because, as mentioned previously, those making the loan decision may not be privy to the conversation. If there is something that might cause concern or is unusual, justify it in your presentation.

5. *Proforma statements:* Offer two years of financial projections. One without the loan proceeds and one with. You can't afford to be grandiose in your view of the future, however the two projections should make clear the benefit(s) of the loan. If that isn't abundantly obvious the bank may not see any reason to make the loan. Then too, banks have listings of industry standards for most every type of business. They will apply those standards to your loan proposal. It is in your interest to be within those standards or be able to explain why you're not.

6. *Repayment schedule:* The keystone to your loan approval or rejection is whether or not the banker feels they are going to be repaid. They want more than a comfortable feeling, they want figures substantiating, at least in their mind, that they have a virtually risk-free loan. Your repayment schedule must coincide with your proforma projections; that is, your statements must prove that you can meet or exceed the loan's repayment demands.

You should also, in this section, offer a worst case scenario. Of course your loan proforma will show you can repay the loan, but what if, for example, the economy goes into a recession? Can you repay the loan then? Don't wait for the banker to ask. Document facts and figures showing you have considered the possibility that circumstances may adversely change and the company has a fall-back position if they do. Most bankers are impressed with such forethought.

7. *Management resumes:* Perhaps, if you're operating a very small business, this will consist of just your resume, but include a current one regardless. Again, those that make the loan decision may not know you, so don't assume anything. Prove to them that you, and others if applicable, know what you're doing and have the educational and experience expertise to ensure continuation of the business and therefore loan repayment. Many good bank loan officers see the bottom line of a small business application in management's abilities. Certainly if it's minimal it will count against you, especially with a Loan and Discount Committee.

8. *Miscellaneous:* This may or may not be applicable to your loan, but if there are positive aspects of your banking relationship that would help your position, use them. For example, items you would want to bring to the attention of the Loan and Discount Committee include: an account relationship for an extended time period; personal accounts at the bank; previously paid-as-agreed credit; use of the bank's payroll service, etc. If there is something positive to be said that didn't fall into the prior seven sections, this is the place.

A loan proposal may sound complicated, but once you start working on it you'll find that's not the case—and I can assure you that you can substantially increase your likelihood of approval with a little preparation. Loan officers don't like to consider loan requests from small business owners who don't seem to have any answers or need to be walked through every loan form. That gives the covert impression that you don't know what you're doing, leading to the overt conclusion that it would be best for the bank to take a pass. Or if you are successful with an approval your loan rate is going to be extremely high. Under these circumstances you can be confident that the bank will demand a personal guarantee and commingling of personal and business assets. We've discussed the necessity of avoiding that occurrence.

After preparing your proposal try and look at it with the banker's mind-set, remembering most loan officers look at a loan application and try and find reasons to reject the loan. See if you have areas that need to be reworked. Surely you don't want to lie or mislead. However, you do want to make the best presentation possible. There are positive and negative ways to say the same thing. Opt for the positive. For those negatives that cannot be avoided, explain them away before the banker ever has a chance to raise questions.

This is a good time to draw your attention to your corporate credit rating. Too many small businesses have no idea what their Dun & Bradstreet report shows, or even if they have one. Check with your credit bureau. Find out what's on your report before the bank orders one for their file. Apply the same criterion for the business that I've outlined with your personal credit report. Don't take chances.

Loan proposal preparation is critical when applying for commercial credit. It can make or break an application. A professional presentation cannot only assure approval, it can reduce up-front costs and give leverage in negotiating a lower interest rate. It can also ease terms and conditions, such as length of repayment and compensating balances. There are many pluses to be garnered by making an effort that culminates in a professional appearing loan proposal.

Many of the principles described above can also be applied to your personal loan applications. While a written proposal may not be necessary, you should, at the least, be able to answer all the questions your banker is sure to ask. Of course, if your personal loan is substantial I recommend a written presentation in addition to the bank's application form(s). Use this outline as a guide.

Whether it's a personal or commercial loan, an impressive loan presentation can dramatically increase your odds of approval while lowering your costs. This holds true with nontraditional lenders too. Even private money likes to feel they are dealing with financially educated individuals, and an authoritative loan proposal conveys that impression.

Compensating Balances

If and when you use your bank for business credit, there is another problem that you must avoid—compensating balances. This banking practice is a supplemental requirement in the granting of some commercial credit; that is, as a requisite to loan approval, the bank requires the borrower to maintain a usually non–interest bearing account balance of (typically) 20 percent of the original loan balance throughout the loan's term. Thus, the customer has actual use of only 80 percent of the amount borrowed. Banks explain compensating balances as a fair method of reciprocity. A closer definition would be extortion.

As questionable as this practice is, there's more to the obvious inequity. And that is, because commercial loans are exempt from the Truth-in-Lending Act, the exact cost of the borrowing may be hidden from the consumer. Let's take a small business single payment loan of $100,000 at 12 percent for one year. The interest cost is $12,000. In this case the 12 percent is a true representation of the actual interest expense. Now let's take the same loan and add a 20 percent compensating balance requirement. What rate of interest will the bank reflect on your loan agreement? The same 12 percent. But, is that accurate?

To find the interest rate you divide the interest expense by the amount borrowed. With no compensating balance the equation looks like this: $12,000 divided by $100,000 = .12, or 12 percent. But, because of compensating balances you only have, in this example, the use of $80,000 ($100,000 minus the compensating balance of $20,000). Let's apply the formula to see what your actual net interest rate is: $12,000 divided by $80,000 = .15, or 15 percent. That's an increase of three percentage points. And what is that increase as a percentage reflection of the interest rate? An amazing 25 percent (three percentage points divided by 12 percent).

If it was just a matter of interest rate and bottom-line return to the bank, the rate, again using our example, would simply be stated as 15 percent, because that's the rate on the money the customer actually gets to use during the loan's term. But that's not the issue. Banks try and use whatever methods they can to conceal needed facts from our review. That's the real issue.

There is another consideration you should know about. As mentioned previously, banks have a daily investment pool called Fed funds. That's where they're going to invest your compensating balances, at a rate anywhere from 6 to 22 percent. Interesting. The bank loans you $100,000 at a dollar cost of $12,000. But, you have to give them back $20,000, interest free, or they won't make the loan. Then they invest that money in a daily investment pool, and, even though they are investing your money, you don't get to share in the results.

Perhaps compensating balances are all right for major corporations, as they have lawyers and accountants that understand their impact on the loan's true cost and the borrower's use and availability of money. But, as the preponderance of banks are of the community, hometown variety, and, by volume, the majority of commercial lending is to small businesses, the bank's method of demanding compensating balances is not in keeping with the image of respectability and service they try and cultivate. A respectable lender doesn't demand compensating balances or withhold loan approval. A respectable lender doesn't withhold the true interest rate from the customer's review.

In larger population centers you have the shopping flexibility of many financial institutions. Under these conditions you should be able to find one that doesn't require compensating balances. Unfortunately, many smaller communities are only serviced by one bank, or there may only be a few in the entire county. If they all demand compensating balances your shopping rights are limited. Of course, you should never forget your other options. In fact, compensating balances may convince you to take advantage of the other numerous lending alternatives.

My use of the word *extortion* doesn't imply that compensating balances are a violation of law. But, like so many of the bank's fees, they are a requirement, without which the bank may refuse you service. That duress is the criterion of my categorization.

Surely, at the very least, compensating balances call into question the issue of fairness, and whether or not government regulation is adequate to protect the small business/commercial consumer. If you're really being charged 15 percent, as in our example, you should be told. Your loan agreement shouldn't say 12 percent.

Pooling Investments and Loans

The smaller investor who tries to take advantage of certain investments that return the highest interest rates is often stymied. The minimum deposit or investment requirement may force you to accept a much lower rate. Banks, brokerage houses, and certain other financial institutions have minimum requirements for a reason. They want to reduce their paperwork and maximize their returns; that is, it's more profitable to service one investor with $100,000 than ten with $10,000 each. Also, lower rates for the masses means higher profits to the bank.

For the purpose of this chapter I am going to use bank Time Certificates of Deposit (TCDs) as examples, not because I recommend them, but rather because so many investors/savers opt for their use and therefore they're understood by most. They are also useful in making the point that the principle of "pooling" can achieve better results than one could accomplish on one's own.

This technique can be used with any investment vehicle. For instance, you've seen the bank ads that outline a TCD of two and one half years at X percent. In most cases there will be a minimum of X dollars. Often, depending on the market, this will be one of the bank's higher available interest rates. To expand the example, if you have over $100,000 the interest rate at the bank will be completely negotiable as to rate and term. This is an example of the benefits of having money; that is, if you have money, it's easier to make more.

Let's say you don't have the bank minimum deposit for the TCD of two and one half years. Does that mean you have to settle for the passbook rate? Absolutely not! Contact friends, relatives, and other interested parties, pool your monies, and make the minimum as a group. All the parties would have to be named on the TCD instrument and sign the appropriate investment agreement (you can make this up yourself), but that's all there is to it. This principle is basically the same in operation as investing in mutual funds. There is nothing to prevent private parties from banding together for the economic benefit of all. It doesn't matter what you invest in, either. Don't limit your thinking to what you personally have to offer financially, forgetting that there is strength and option flexibility in numbers. That's true whether you're talking about people or dollars.

To be safe with your investment pool, I have to caution, be precise with your documentation. This need not be complicated for it to be legal. Simply state in the document's body the intentions of all the signers. This should include all eventualities such as the death of one party, withdrawal rights, borrowing rights, sale rights, etc. Have each party sign and retain a copy.

Investment pools have unlimited potential and can be a valuable tool in the arsenal of the smaller investor/saver. But what about that other important aspect of financial life, namely borrowing?

As stated earlier, I feel that the correct way to borrow is perhaps as or more important than saving. Why? Because most owe more than they have saved. When you take into account mortgages, business borrowings, and loans for personal needs, that is true for all but the most affluent person. It is very possible, using the pool concept, to lower your borrowing costs. If you're in the market for a mortgage, start looking for others (a local newspaper ad seems to work well here) in the market that are willing to band together for their mortgaging needs. Then make a presentation to the local financial institutions for ten or so mortgages instead of only one. Obviously you want people who have good credit ratings, but you get the point. If you screen your partners correctly and have, instead of just one $100,000 mortgage request, a million dollars' worth of grade-A borrowers to offer the bank, private lender, brokerage house, etc., you are in a great negotiating position.

This will hold true for any type of loan. If you're a doctor looking for expansion capital, start looking around. There are other doctors in the same process at the same time. Work together and make a package proposal. You will still have an individual loan, but the initial presentation will save you interest points, closing costs, and most assuredly you can negotiate the lowest rate possible. Lenders always need quality borrowers. Use their requirements to your advantage. Group discounts are available to borrowers.

Organization and presentation are the keys to getting things done. Designate someone as the spokesperson and allow him or her to present the individual documentation that makes up the group's request. I cannot stress enough that this is virtually an untapped market. Yet I can assure you that this concept works. Remember, as with all borrowings, you should shop around with the package at a minimum of three lending outlets!

Whether you're investing or borrowing you cannot afford to overlook the benefits of pooling your resources. If you're investing it will allow you better interest rate returns and access to vehicles you otherwise would be denied. If you're borrowing it will save you up-front costs and points. It will reduce your interest rate costs yearly and improve your cash flow. In either case you're not tied to the other pool members in any way other than purpose. Your money is still your money and your loan is still your loan. None of your pool partners, assuming that your documentation is done properly, can adversely affect your deposits or loan. This is just one creative way to make the most of your financial future, and beat the bank's saving/lending structure designed to pay the small investor/saver the least, while charging them the most when they borrow.

Knowing How Much Is Safe to Borrow

There is no bigger credit pitfall then allowing yourself to become overextended. Your bank, on the other hand, not only has little concern in this regard, they want you borrowed to the hilt and beyond. Especially if you are using an installment loan or credit card as your lending vehicle. The bank's return on personal loans is so huge that the consumer's financial well-being is trampled by the banker's lust for maximum profits. Your banker, if he is to meet the service intent of his bank's charter, should be offering loans that are prudent for both the bank and the customer. Unfortunately, many bankers ignore their guidance responsibility and focus only on the positive impact your loan will have on the bank's bottom line.

Banks, when dealing in loan types that have lower returns (mortgages for example), are very conservative in their lending decisions. With loans that have monstrous returns (credit cards for instance), they are truly liberal. This ludicrous disparity of concern is directly proportionate to the bank's profit margin on each loan type. If you're buying a highly secured home mortgage at 12 percent they run you through the wringer and want every i dotted and t crossed. If you're using a credit card at 22 percent they couldn't care less what you buy, when you buy it, and/or if you can afford it.

The bank's misplaced regard for your credit abilities shouldn't cloud your decisions. You must know, based on your ability to repay, what your borrowing parameters are. Don't base that answer on limits set by the bank. Their vested interest(s) are a reflection of their profit expectations. You need an answer based on your wants tempered by your financial realities.

While I am against borrowing for most of the normal reasons, let's assume here that you have a legitimate reason for purchasing money. There is a method of ascertaining if your borrowing is in line with your income. This rule-of-thumb should be applied without reservation or rationalization to be effective. I tell you up-front that many will be shocked to find they're woefully overextended.

Take your after-tax income, subtract your housing and auto expense, and multiply the answer by 12 percent (.12). It's that simple. The answer indicates the total outstanding additional debt you can comfortably afford. Most family budgets will fail this test as we as a nation have been conditioned to excessive credit obligations. But that doesn't mean it's right. If you're overextended it's time for some changes, no matter how inconvenient.

Let's look at an example. A family with an after-tax income of $30,000, and a housing expense (take into account the rent or mortgage, taxes, maintenance, and insurance) of $750 per month, or $9,000 per year, and a car expense of $250 a month, or $3,000 per year, should have an additional debt not to exceed $2,160 ($30,000 − 9,000 − 3,000 = 18,000 X .12 = 2,160). That debt ceiling should include all your other obligations, regardless of how or why they are originated.

Surprised? Think the total is too small? It's not. If you're above your limit you shouldn't panic. However, do take this exercise as a blueprint for change.

How serious is this principle of understanding the relationship of debt and your ability to repay? It is critical. A case in point is made every time another former millionaire files bankruptcy. They had income, they had assets—what they didn't have was control of their debt.

And your bank's role in all this? Contrary to their image, they are one of the major purveyors of easy, overpriced credit. As long as their return is excessive they will ignore the basic lending principles of the Five Cs of credit. They will also ignore their responsibility to provide guidance for their clients. When we go to other professionals we expect advice that is appropriate for our circumstances; that is, the best service at the lowest possible cost. But the bank does just the opposite. They offer the worst possible solution, high priced credit, for the very people that, for their own good, should be denied. Far too many banks will be more than happy to extend you expensive credit in excess of what is safe for your financial particulars. While interest rates should be a reflection of exposure to risk, your credit limit shouldn't be set by the same criterion. And your banker knows that. Yet, they are willing to ignore what is best for you if their profit is large enough.

Protect yourself. No matter what you pay for money you shouldn't exceed what you can afford. Don't let any lender ruin your future by offering you high-priced, easy money. And even when you get a good deal on credit don't borrow more than you can afford.

Understanding the Language of Loans

Once your loan is approved you have one final important concern, a concern that most unfortunately ignore: understanding what you're about to sign. Few bother to read the fine print of a loan agreement. They trust their banker. Or they know they stand little chance of deciphering the bank legalese, so they just give up. Your banker, of course, doesn't want you to read and understand the technicalities of your obligation. Entering into an agreement that you don't understand is bad enough. Doing so because the other party, in this case your bank, made every effort to ensure you couldn't, is quite another.

Lest you think I am exaggerating to make a point, let's review a few loan clauses typically, or historically, included in bank lending contracts.

Bank/Legalese: *To guarantee payment hereof, the undersigned jointly and severally irrevocably authorize any attorney or court of record to appear for any one or more of them in such court in term or vacation, after default in payment hereof and confess a judgment without process in favor of the creditor hereof for such an amount as may appear unpaid.*

Plain English Interpretation: If the bank decides to sue due to a delinquency you've agreed to let them win even if you had a perfectly valid reason for not paying. Believe it or not, you've also agreed to the obvious ethical conflict of having the bank represent you and the bank in court.

Bank/Legalese: *Each of us individually and severally waives any and all benefit or relief from all exemptions or moratoriums to which the signers or any of them may be entitled under the laws of this or any other state now in force or hereafter passed against this debt.*

Plain English Interpretation: If you are in default you have given the bank the right to take property that, without this waiver, may have been protected from seizure.

Bank/Legalese: *We severally authorize and direct our employers or future employers to pay a part of our salary, wages, commissions, or other compensation for services to the said assignee and release such employers or any future employers from all liability to us on account of any and all monies paid in accordance with the terms hereof. We severally give and grant unto the said assignee full power and authority to demand, receive, and receipt for the same of any part thereof in any of our names.*

Plain English Interpretation: If you are delinquent you have given the bank the right to immediately demand a portion of your salary to satisfy their debt. You will not argue about it regardless of the circumstances.

Bank/Legalese: *If this agreement is referred to any attorney for collection due to default or breach of any promise or provision hereunder by debtor, debtor agrees to pay reasonable attorney fees plus court costs.*

Plain English Interpretation: If the bank sues you've agreed to pay their lawyer.

Bank/Legalese: *Default in the payment of any installment of the principal or charges hereof or any part of either shall, at the option of the holder hereof, render the entire balance, principal and interest, at once due and payable.*

Plain English Interpretation: If you miss a single monthly payment the bank can call the whole loan due immediately.

Bank/Legalese: *The undersigned jointly and severally agree that the lender may communicate with any persons whatsoever in relation to this obligation involved, or its delinquency, in an effort to obtain cooperation to help relative to the collection or payment thereof.*

Plain English Interpretation: If you are delinquent the bank can tell your friends and relatives.

These clauses may or may not be used by your bank. However, they are fairly common and are only a small representation of the many potentially damaging clauses used on varying loan contracts. Some states concerned with consumer rights have limited the types and/or the scope of loan clauses a bank may use.

I offer these examples to make a point. Signing a loan that waives virtually all your rights as a credit consumer is a huge financial mistake. Yet, almost all banks do everything they can to ensure that's exactly what you do. Sadly, they are not even aboveboard in their tactics. They do so in the fine print and in bank/legalese in the hope that you will never realize, until it's too late, that you've little or no recourse in a loan dispute.

Unfortunately, this type of hidden abuse is fairly common within the banking community, which is just one more reason to shop your lending needs. You must thoroughly review every loan contract prior to agreeing to its terms, so if a dispute arises you will, at the very least, understand your options. Try and find a bank or other credit outlet that offers a balanced loan contract. A creditor has every right to try and protect its position, but it should do so openly and fairly. Too many banks have decided bank/legalese better serves their purposes.

Bank Savings—
They Aren't

How the Bank Makes Your Savings
Interest Disappear

Most of us, when reviewing a savings investment opportunity, look for the best interest rate or return. Little else is considered. For instance, if Bank X has a 10 percent interest rate for its two-year TCD, and Bank Y offers 10.5 percent for the same certificate, we invest with Bank Y. Very few people bother to ascertain how banks arrive at their interest rates, that is, what method of interest computation they use. Without that vital piece of information we cannot actually compare anything, because we don't have the critical fact that would allow for an intelligent saving decision.

As hard as this may be for you to believe, it is possible that Bank X actually has the better interest rate return. How? For the sake of argument let's say that Bank X uses day-of-deposit-to-day-of-withdrawal interest, compounded and paid daily. Bank Y is on FIFO (First In/First Out), compounded and paid quarterly. Further, let's assume it has a full-quarter requirement on all deposits. This means all monies have to be on deposit for the full ninety days to receive interest—many, many banks have this requirement.

It should be immediately obvious that daily interest is better than quarterly interest as your interest starts compounding additional interest that much faster. Also, Bank X gives you flexibility in that no matter when you make a withdrawal you will have received interest for the entire time the bank used your money.

Bank Y on the other hand, even though it offered a higher rate, would pay you interest provided you leave the money on deposit the full quarter. If you make a withdrawal on the seventy-fifth day you lose seventy-five days' worth of interest up front.

There are more important considerations. Let's go further and look at an example account at Bank Y to make the point.

Balance on 1st day of quarter	$5,000
Deposit on 15th day of quarter	2,500
Balance to date	7,500
Deposit on 30th day of quarter	7,000
Balance to date	14,500
Withdrawal on 60th day of quarter	2,500
Balance to date	12,000
Withdrawal on 80th day of quarter	3,000
Balance to date	9,000
Deposit on 87th day of quarter	3,000
Balance on last day of quarter	12,000

Now, assuming our example interest rate of 10.5 percent for Bank Y, what do you believe would be the interest earned during the quarter?

I'll give you some additional information that may help. (1) The lowest balance during the month was $5,000. (2) The average balance during the month was $10,683.33. (3) Using the the bank's daily investment interest rate (the Fed fund rate) of 12 percent (this rate could be substantially higher), the bank earned $316.11 on the account during the quarter. That should be enough information.

Clearly the bank uses every opportunity to maximize its use of your money. Most of you would agree that this account deserves interest based on the information I've outlined. You're right in principle, but wrong nevertheless.

Bank Y, with its .5 percentage point higher rate than Bank X will pay the customer *no* interest for the quarter. That's because none of the deposits will earn anything as they will not meet the full-quarter requirement. The original balance of $5,000 will also lose its interest as, using FIFO, all withdrawals during the month come out of that original balance, and since the withdrawals exceeded that balance it earns nothing. Pretty simple isn't it? Thousands, perhaps millions, of bank customers earn nothing on their savings because banks are allowed to use varying methods to compute interest on savings. Because of that government-approved deception, banks devised numerous mutated savings interest computation methods that would, whenever possible, completely negate your saving's return.

Remember, in dealing with your bank, all things are not as they appear. You have to ensure that your bank is paying day-of-deposit-to-day-of-withdrawal interest, compounded and paid daily. If they don't, find another bank. Anything less and you're being cheated. Do you doubt that? Compare the same principle to when the bank borrows from us. Don't forget, that's what it is doing when we make a deposit. It is borrowing our money. And yet, as discussed throughout this book, banks have hold times, extra service fees, varying methods of interest computations, etc., all designed to separate us from our funds. See what happens when we borrow money from them. Surely they play by the same rules.

Not so.

When we borrow from them we start paying interest on the day the loan is signed. In practice they may not actually pay any money out for your loan proceeds for many, many days. Let me give you an example. You buy a car and finance it at your bank. You sign the papers on Friday late in the afternoon. You pick up the car and pay for it with the bank's cashier's check on Saturday. The dealership puts it through their bank late on Monday. The check doesn't clear back to the originating bank until perhaps Friday. A full week has elapsed. The bank hasn't actually loaned you one dollar until the check clears, but you've paid them a full week's interest. On a $10,000 car loan at 10 percent simple interest, you were charged $19.18 in interest during that time. During that same time the bank used that same money as an investment for their profit. At a 12 percent Fed fund rate the bank made an additional $23.01 while that money waited for your loan check to clear. Granted, these aren't huge amounts, but they add up. Multiply this example times the number of daily bank loans and you have millions being spent by the consumer for absolutely nothing. Substantial loan interest is being paid by the consumer long before the bank expends any actual lending dollars.

At the very least this savings/loan parallel should show you that banks don't play fair. With your savings you are denied monies owed you, and with a bank loan you are perhaps charged interest before there is actually any real loan disbursement. If banks are going to make all the rules, they should be the same on both sides of the equation.

Now that I've put you on guard, let's proceed with another question/example to make another salient point. In today's market, what rate of savings interest do you need just to break even with a bank-type saving investment? As of this writing inflation is at 4.5 percent. Let's not forget the tax consideration. If you're in the 28 percent bracket you need another 1.54 percent to break even (28 percent of the present passbook savings rate). That's a total of 6.04 percent. As of this writing, regular savings and Notice of Withdrawal (NOW) accounts are paying approximately 5.50 percent. That means you are losing money with those accounts every year. At present many TCDs are also losers!

I realize that this is a simplistic example, but then sometimes those are the best. The point to my second example is that even in the best of times most bank savings investments don't actually break even! You can imagine the impact of runaway inflation! In that environment bank returns are too ludicrous even to be considered, and that narrows the field even further. Bank savings accounts are highly suspect in terms of return on their face. Add to that the bank's way of computing our savings interest and you seriously have to question the advisability of any form of bank savings vehicle.

The bottom line in all this is that it is imperative that you consider all avenues in your investment choices. If you consider only your local bank you could be making a costly mistake.

Let's review two specific considerations:

1. When you compare savings interest rates make sure you are comparing likes that allow for such a comparison. They all should use day-of-deposit-to-day-of-withdrawal interest, compounded and paid daily. Once you've located institutions that offer that method you then can compare rates for the most advantageous.

2. After arriving at your savings/investment choice, apply the other considerations, such as the inflation rate, taxes, etc., and then see if the choice still makes sense. More often than not it leaves the bank out of the running.

You have to ignore the norms and realize how the game is played. Understanding the nuances of certain vehicles is an important cog in that thought process; that is, even if you use a bank vehicle, you then have to decipher and understand the specifics of that choice.

I hope my examples once again made clear that banks are not to be trusted. Why? Because they will take as much of your money as they can, and they do so by contriving circumstances you can't control or understand. They take bank savings, a questionable investment in the first place, and turn it into a complete, unabashed rip-off by using interest computation methods that deny us our rightful savings interest.

There are times, such as when interest rates are exceptionally high, and circumstances, perhaps for certain elderly people who need additional reliable monthly income, that bank savings are worthy of consideration. But at all times, you must know what to ask for. Settle for nothing less than you deserve!

Bank IRAs Are a Bad Investment

When Individual Retirement Accounts (IRAs) became law, they were lauded for personal financial planning. Congress trumpeted their benefits. Banks lined up to "compete" for their deposits. Investment counselors emphasized their necessity.

I believe that IRAs are, at best, not all they promised. The

Tax Reform Act of 1986 proved that point conclusively. At worst, a bank IRA could be the most unrewarding investment you ever make.

Planning for your retirement is to be applauded. Those who don't are making a terrible mistake. Those who are depending on Social Security for a financially secure retirement are in for a shock, as the system is statistically bankrupt. You must make your own provisions. But are IRAs the best choice?

You make two major assumptions when you start an IRA: The tax structure will remain unchanged and your interest will outstrip inflation. But how reliable are these assumptions? First, because of tax *reform*, we now know that Congress is not above changing the rules whenever it suits its purposes. Twenty years from now is it unlikely that Congress won't highly tax the billions of IRA deposits? It is more than likely; it's probable.

Everyone has an estimate about future inflation rates, but you're not likely to get a pessimistic one from your bank. Inflation, according to the Government Accounting Office, assuming it extrapolates historically, will, in twenty-five years, give an IRA with a balance of over $1 million the buying power of only $50,000. That could be less than your contributions!

The point is, the IRA concept needs further review to see if it fits your anticipated financial needs. There are other avenues, investments, etc., all of which, even after taxes, could return more to the retiree. I believe these should be considered before blindly accepting an IRA as the answer to your retirement.

Nonetheless, millions of people are investing in IRAs. A large portion of those investors are investing in bank IRAs, and few of them really know what they've bought. Look around. Check your documentation. Make sure you understand the nuances of your plan. Don't wait until you're ready for your first monthly check to discover you didn't understand what you signed up for twenty, thirty years ago.

My complaint with bank IRAs is two-fold, beginning with their interest rate returns. Financial institutions sell their IRAs through fear and planned misunderstandings. They stress that you need a retirement plan above and beyond Social Security. So far they are correct. Then they say they're there to help. Nothing could be further from the truth. Banks and savings and loan associations love IRAs for one reason and one reason only. They are "cheap money." Their interest rate returns are historically one to three percentage points below those of other available market IRA vehicles. Of course they remind us that their accounts are insured by the FDIC and other IRAs are not. I direct your attention to the chapter that reviews the FDIC for my sentiments regarding its "insurance."

These below-market rates being offered through banks can be even worse than advertised (see the preceding section, "How the Bank Makes Your Savings Interest Disappear"). Also, depending on your plan, that method may be changed at the bank's discretion. You should note that bank IRA interest rates are not uniform; realizing that makes it mandatory that you determine what method your bank uses. You want day-of-deposit-to-day-of-withdrawal interest, compounded and paid daily. If your bank doesn't offer that method you are not receiving the maximum IRA interest benefit.

The trouble is, most investors don't understand how the bank reduces your net return and/or they think only of the tax consideration of the account. Banks depend on that. They want you thinking taxes. They want you thinking retirement. They don't want you thinking interest rate or how they compute that rate. They want you to continually contribute to their IRA pool of cheap money. The fact is, if you want an IRA you should get the best interest rate possible. If you choose a bank IRA you are possibly losing one to three percentage points you could have earned through a more profitable market IRA. In later years that will mean thousands of dollars lost every year.

The crux of the issue? If you believe an IRA is your retirement answer compare market IRAs for the best rate. If you believe bank IRAs are best, make sure your bank's method of interest computation is in accordance with my recommendation.

The second concern I have regarding bank IRAs is associated with the banks' selling techniques. There is a great deal of misinformation spread about tax benefits and the balances actually insured by the FDIC. Look at the following table.

HOW AN INDIVIDUAL RETIREMENT ACCOUNT GROWS

Age	Total Deposit at Age 65 (at $2,000/yr.)	8%		11%	
		Value at Age 65	Approx. Mo. Payment at Age 65*	Value at Age 65	Approx. Mo. Payment at Age 65*
20	$90,000	$961,713	$7,753	$2,845,142	$28,656
25	80,000	632,554	5,099	1,621,049	16,327
30	70,000	413,125	3,330	920,124	9,267
35	60,000	266,845	2,151	518,769	5,225
40	50,000	169,330	1,365	288,950	2,910
45	40,000	104,323	841	157,354	1,584
50	30,000	60,986	491	82,001	825
55	20,000	32,097	258	38,853	391
60	10,000	12,838	103	14,147	142

*Based on 22-year life, including survivor benefits. Federal regulations require substantial penalties for early withdrawal of Individual Retirement Accounts.

Note: This table is for purpose of illustration only.

Interest rates are subject to change and will vary over long periods of time. Specific rates will be quoted at the time the account is opened and reviewed regularly in the best interest of the depositor.

This is an actual table used by a bank to promote IRA deposits.

Some of the numbers are rather impressive. Unfortunately they don't mean anything. They do, however, bring up some interesting facts. First, the bank is basing its monthly retirement payments on the assumption that the person holding the account lives twenty-two years after he or she begins receiving disbursements. Not many of us are going to live until eighty-seven, which means the monthly disbursements, if they are to have any basis in reality, are going to have to be accelerated considerably. Even at that (using the bank's figures), you can see that if you start its 8 percent IRA at age twenty, when payments begin you will have a monthly income of $7,753 or a yearly income of $93,036. You know what that means! Taxes. So much for "being taxed at a lower rate," which the banks so frequently advertise and discuss. They give the impression that, since you will no longer be employed, your tax rate will be reduced, when in fact your IRA payments may put you in a higher tax bracket. Of course, you'll pay taxes regardless of which IRA you choose. My point is that banks are not adequately informing the public regarding the complexity of an IRA account. Sure, some of the technical aspects are there in the paperwork, but what person not endowed with an accounting and law degree can understand the bankerese?

However, that's still not the main point. I use the chart so you can see why you should ignore government deposit insurance when considering an IRA. If you believe in FDIC insurance, you'll be shocked to realize that all the bank's advertising charts indicate that only a very small portion of your IRA deposits will be covered! I have never seen information to that effect, but that doesn't surprise me. It's just another example of banks telling only the part of the truth that suits their purposes. When they want your deposits they bring your attention to the insurance factor. Millions of people will deposit money only in an FDIC financial institution. But when these institutions advertise IRA accounts and their huge balances after twenty or thirty years, they forget to mention that only a small portion ($100,000) of the account will be insured.

This chart shows balances that are impressive. In one case the 8 percent balance is $961,713. It fails to mention that $861,713 will be uninsured. The 11 percent example is even more frightening! At the very time you will want to have the security of the FDIC insurance, it will be virtually nonexistent.

I don't think much of this kind of insurance for a variety of reasons. But it means a lot to many people, who give up additional interest for the security they perceive. In the case of a bank IRA, they are giving up a lot of money for nothing.

Take that balance of $961,713. If that bank IRA pays one percentage point less than the market IRA interest rates it means the customer loses $9,617.13 in the interest differential. If we use the 11 percent figure shown, the differential one percentage point loss on your $2,845,142.00 is $28,451.42. At three percentage points the differential loss on the 8 percent account is $28,851.39. On the 11 percent account the loss is $85,354.26! And that's only for one year.

The point of this exercise? IRAs need to be reviewed in depth before you invest. If, after determining your needs, you still want to invest I doubt that you should consider an IRA at your bank. Their rates are almost always below market, substantially below market. Even a one percentage point differential can be costly as I've shown. People allow the differential either because they don't understand the account or they want the FDIC insurance. But, you could *lose* almost as much in one year's interest, due to the rate differential, as the FDIC presently will insure.

Retirement planning is essential. One cannot overstate its importance. That's why you should investigate all your IRA options. If you do a thorough review I believe you'll find that a bank IRA is the least acceptable alternative.

Bank "Services"

Bank Overdrafts

If you overdraft your checking account you've committed a misdemeanor under the Deceptive Practices Act. Strictly interpreted, even if you cover the check before it clears, you still, at the time you wrote the check, broke the law. Obviously this strict interpretation is seldom enforced. If it was half the country would be in jail. But enforcement of the law is not the point. I highly recommend that you never purposely overdraft your account. Not because it's against the law, but rather because it's a shoddy way to do business.

I am ignoring, of course, those who overdraft their account for the purpose of fraud. That is a criminal act and criminals should be prosecuted.

For most, however, overdrafting an account is usually an honest error. Maybe you made a mistake in adding up your checkbook. Maybe you got to the bank late with your deposit.

There are many legitimate ways an overdraft can happen, but that is not the issue.

The point is the relationship between you and your bank and how that affects the "service" of overdrafts.

Up front, in fairness to the bank, it has to be stated that when you overdraft your account you cause extra work for the bank staff, as well as extra bank expense. The bank has a right to be compensated even if your overdraft was accidental. That's not arguable.

How much do they spend processing an overdraft (OD)? Most bank cost-analysis surveys indicate a cost of 35¢ to 75¢. I believe it's closer to a dollar, based on the following:

Computer cost per OD	$0.25
Employee's processing cost	0.46
Mailing cost of OD notice	0.29
Total	$1.00

The average OD charge is presently $25 per check. That means those banks are making a percentage return on their "investment" (actual overdraft processing cost) of 2,500 percent. That seems a little high to me. Especially in light of the fact that they are willing to pay us only 5.5 percent on our NOW accounts!

As bad as that is, some banks are charging $50 per check! That means if you have three checks bounce in the same day, you are charged $150. At $50, the bank makes a return of 5,000 percent. Although they incur no additional expense for multiple-check ODs on the same day, some banks charge you for each check! Their returns become astronomical!

Although bankers would like us to think of OD fees as their protection against returned check losses, in fact ODs are one of banks' major, major income producers. That should give you an indication of their true intentions in assessing unreasonable, unjustifiable fees for sending our checks back through the clearing system. Those fees are not for the purpose of discouraging customer OD abuse. They are generating huge profits! Profits that make the return on the most profitable loan in the bank's loan portfolio pale by comparison. Banks, contrary to their rhetoric, *want* you to overdraft your account. And the more the better. Unless they decide to pay the overdraft, which in most instances is highly unlikely, the bank has no exposure to loss. Therefore each overdraft becomes almost pure profit.

There is more to the story. With the advent of deregulation most banks have gone to a ten- to fourteen-day hold on your deposits. Some use calendar days, others, business days. That means even though 90 percent of all checks deposited in this country on any given day clear within the first forty-eight hours, the bank will not allow you to draw against those funds. Bankers say they need this hold time to make sure the checks in our deposits are "good." That's nonsense. Only 1 percent of checks are ever returned to the bank for any reason, and only 1 percent of that 1 percent are ever returned with no bank recourse.

Additionally, some will not pay you interest until the hold time elapses. Since the bank has daily investment opportunities, this hold policy means that we are forced to make them an interest-free loan for the time between when the check actually clears and when they will allow us to draw against those funds. I feel obligated to repeat again. That means families, even families which perhaps survive on poverty-level incomes, are forced to make interest-free loans to banks that in some cases are worth billions of dollars! I believe that is morally reprehensible by any standard. Right now there is a move to change the hold policy by law, but it is too little, too late. Banks have been getting away with this for years. Billions of consumer dollars have been lost. Frankly, based on its long-standing record of doing the banker's bidding I have little faith that Congress will now begin working to help the financial consumer. Consequently, I don't expect any change in law to square with the facts, even if the banks are forced to make less exorbitant profits.*

Banks would like us to think of these long hold times as a protective measure, but once again they are misleading us. They are creating ODs when in fact there are none. Because they won't let us draw against the funds, even though they are collected, you have to pay an OD charge. Sometimes you are just charged an uncollected funds fee of, say, $10. You may have thousands of dollars in your account, but because of the bank's unreasonable hold policy you have to pay an OD charge!

*On September 1, 1988, the Expedited Funds Availability Act went into effect. Under the new law, next business-day credit is given to funds deposited by cash, direct deposit, electronic transfers, cashier's, certified, and government checks, or checks drawn on the same financial institution. Local checks must receive credit by the third business day. Nonlocal checks receive credit as of the seventh business day. Moreover, banks can add up to four additional business days to the hold time if: (1) they believe a check you deposit will not be paid; (2) you deposit checks totaling more than $5,000.00 on any one day; (3) you redeposit a check that has been returned unpaid; (4) you have overdrawn your account repeatedly in the last six months; or (5) there is an emergency, such as failure of communications or computer equipment. There are numerous added contingencies if your account is less than thirty days old. On September 1, 1990, a permanent, slightly differing collection schedule took effect. Ask your bank for a copy of the changes.

This law still doesn't give the consumers fair access to their money. Banks continue to receive interest-free loans from their depositors. In addition, three or seven business days can easily, with weekends and holidays, turn into five or ten calendar days. Add the numerous discretionary exceptions and, in many instances, the new hold times exceed the old requirements. Consumers need to look at the intent of this law by remembering that almost all checks deposited clear within the first forty-eight hours; your funds are still available to the bank for their investment purposes days or weeks before the new hold has elapsed. This is just one more case in which Congress has given legitimacy to a highly questionable banking practice.

There is more bad news. Many banks compound the problem because they don't have an on-premise computer (most community banks are in this category). That means they have to ship out the day's work for processing. To accomplish that with a limited time span, they have a cutoff time for all transactions. Usually it's around 2 P.M. That means if you make a deposit after that time it goes on the next day's business. Many sections of the country still have banks that close one day midweek, normally Wednesday. Consider the following scenario.

You make a deposit on Tuesday, after 2 P.M. That, because of the bank's schedule, makes it Wednesday's work. But the bank is closed Wednesday, which means your deposit gets pushed back until Thursday. And that means it doesn't actually get posted on the bank records until Friday morning. If you've got checks that clear on Thursday, you're out of luck. (This, of course, doesn't even take into account hold times.) Again, the bank is creating ODs and you have to pay for it.

These practices make the banks millions each week. They earn fees for a nonexistent OD "service," and in addition they use our money for their investments.

It's not enough to complain. I'm giving you a method to combat this situation. Specifically:

1. Know and understand your bank's hold policy.

2. If you receive an OD notice when there really wasn't one, demand that the bank refund your OD charge and that it send an apology letter to each person who received your returned checks. You shouldn't let the bank's hold policy damage your credit rating with others. If the bank will not respond, take it to small claims court. Unfortunately, most people don't bother, which is one of the reasons this practice continues.

3. If you feel particularly abused, consider a class-action suit. You would need to find an aggressive, contingency-fee lawyer. This approach, more than any other, holds promise for true reform. Such a suit against a major money center bank could be worth millions to the class. Only when banks cannot afford this shameful practice will they stop. Class-action suits, for this and other abuses, is a means to that end.

To summarize, overdrafting your account is wrong if done intentionally, and even if you made an honest mistake you should be assessed a fair fee for the extra work you caused. But overdraft fees charged by most banks cannot be justified by cost analysis. Furthermore, a large percentage of ODs and uncollected funds charges are created by the bank. We should never have to pay a fee under those circumstances!

Overdraft Checking

Overdraft checking allows you to write checks for more than you have in your account without the fear that your check will be returned. At most institutions the overdraft checking interest rate, although it varies from bank to bank, is lower than most loan vehicles, whether straight consumer loans or credit card transactions. (The reason being, your overdraft checking line is preapproved, so there is no loan application expense incurred by the bank, and too, there are no documentation costs as the necessary legal paperwork was completed at the time your credit line was approved and your check becomes the loan disbursement.) At face value, overdraft checking doesn't sound too bad. It protects you from the embarrassment of an overdraft return, the expense of an overdraft, and the usually high cost of most bank lending. Unfortunately, you have to delve deeper to truly determine the cost/benefit ratio of the service.

Most overdraft checking plans work in one of two ways (or a combination of both). One plan is that the bank will deposit an amount to the next hundred dollars that is required to cover your overdraft. For example, if you overdraft your account $105 the bank will deposit $200 in your account. Naturally, you're charged interest on the higher amount. In this case $200, even though $95 of the loan ($200 − $105) will remain in your checking account. Until you write a check against the difference the bank will be using the $95 for their investment purposes, notwithstanding the fact that you're paying interest on it. Let's say the bank charges 12 percent (many banks charge more) on their overdraft protection accounts. That's 1 percent per month, which is certainly less expensive than a bank credit card that may run as high as 22 percent. But, are you really paying 12 percent on the amount you actually needed to borrow? No, of course not. Your monthly cost for the $200 is $2 at 12 percent.

Remember, you only needed to borrow $105. The $2 bank charge is equal to a 22.8 percent charge on that amount ($2 divided by $105 X 12). You see, by depositing money you don't need the bank almost doubles your expense. As is so often the case when you deal with banks, you have to understand the entire transaction, even unstated nuances, before you can determine your net cost.

The other overdraft checking method used is an interest rate—let's use 12 percent again—charged by the bank plus a transaction fee for every overdraft check that causes a loan to be made to your account. Here too the fees vary. Suppose the bank has a $1 fee for each check. What does that do to your actual cost? Staying with our example of a $105 overdraft, your interest rate cost for the month, assuming this bank simply loans you the exact amount you are overdrafted, will be $1.05. But to that we have to add $1, so your total charge is $2.05, or an equivalent interest rate of 23.4 percent ($2.05 divided by $105 X 12). It should be noted that a per check fee will have less of an interest rate impact the more money you borrow, however, the majority of such transactions are for smaller amounts. Regardless of the actual interest rate per transaction, you will be paying more than what you thought you would be charged.

Now let's combine the two approaches and see how ridiculously costly this can become. Again, you overdraft your account $105. The bank deposits $200, and they have a $1 per check transaction fee. The stated interest rate (APR) on your loan agreement is 12 percent. In this case your actual interest charge for the month is $2. To that we have to add the $1 transaction fee, for a total of $3. A $3 monthly charge for a loan of $105 is equal to an interest rate expense of 34.3 percent ($3 divided by $105 X 12), or almost triple what the bank is advertising.

All of a sudden this service doesn't sound so appealing does it? That's because it's not. Certainly there are instances where one would want such protection, and like credit cards, if you're going to use it, do so for convenience only. Don't actually borrow money using your overdraft protection account. The bank would like you to do just that as they know their net return is in excess of their stated APR. This "cheap" method of borrowing, as I've shown above, isn't cheap at all. That's why banks would like you to roll-over your loan month after month. To that end, many banks will even debit your checking account for your minimum payment amount so you won't have to be bothered paying the bill. That sounds good, but the bank has ulterior motives. Since their bill paying service only pays the minimum payment it ensures that you will have a loan balance next month whether you make additional purchases of money or not. And that same balance will be subject to another interest charge next month. They would rather that you never pay off the balance, which is the philosophy they have with credit card balances. They want you to borrow as much as they think you can conceivably pay back, and then keep paying on that debt forever. A revolving line of overdraft protection should never become a permanent debt.

Overdraft checking sounds like a bargain. It's not. It is, in many cases, nothing more than an expensive way to get deeper in debt. My main objection is not the concept, but rather that it appears to be one thing when it's actually something quite different. Anytime you enter into a lending transaction that may cost you three times what you thought, you've got a problem.

When you remember that many of the overdrafts the bank will be protecting you from are caused by their unreasonable hold policy on your deposits, the hidden cost of this service becomes even more objectionable.

Your Safe Deposit Box—It Isn't

How safe is a safe deposit box?

Many of you may expect total security. The opposite is true. Safe deposit boxes offer virtually no safety. In fact, in some cases having a safe deposit box will actually hinder the safety of your finances.

This is another perfect case in point of banks offering a service that is not what it purports to be; that is, the consumer does not receive what he thought he purchased.

Most bankers, when asked about their safe deposit function, will tell you that their vault is impervious to theft, fire, flood, and that no one, without your permission, can enter the box. Further, should the impossible happen, your contents are insured by the bank's insurance company, so there is no reason to worry. If you doubt this response, go to your bank and ask.

If you believe your banker, a safe deposit box sounds like a reasonable answer to the problem of safety for your valuables. It's too bad that's not the case. Using a series of questions and answers, let's dissect the numerous potential problems with a safe deposit box.

1. *Are bank vaults impervious to break-ins?* As substantial as bank vaults are, a professional burglar can always get in if he wants to. Recently a major money center bank in San Francisco was broken into. The thieves tunneled under all the security devices. Once inside they short-circuited the electronic security. This bank's vault and security was far in excess of what most community banks offer, and yet it was totally compromised. Having gained entry to the vault, a burglar can pop a safe deposit box in about ten seconds using an ordinary screwdriver. That's what happened in this case.

Obviously, then, a safe deposit box offers little substantive security. The only reason your bank's vault hasn't been victimized is that no professional thief has made an attempt. When and if he does it's likely he will be successful. So, the next time you get a warm feeling of security looking at your bank's vault, don't. It's more show than security.

2. *Are bank vaults safe from fire and flood?* Absolutely not! A flood would not be too damaging under most circumstances, since the contents of the boxes would still be intact. Damaged maybe, but not lost. Fire, however, can be a major problem. Although the vault would normally be the last to burn, it will, if the fire exceeds the vault's fire rating, burn. Therefore the contents of your safe deposit box may be lost if they are vulnerable to high temperatures. Stamp collections, paper money, important documents, etc., will almost always be consumed.

3. *Is it true that no one can enter your box without permission?* No. For instance, if you have an unpaid delinquent tax obligation, the government, state or federal, can obtain a warrant to invade your safe deposit box and confiscate its contents to pay its claim. The bank will have no choice but to comply with the warrant. If your safe deposit box key is not available, or you will not voluntarily surrender it, the bank will have the lock drilled to assist the court officer. Then it will send you the bill for the drilling expense and a new lock for the box.

In many states if you and your spouse (or someone else) have equal access to a safe deposit box and one of you dies, the bank will seal the box and not let the other enter under any circumstances. Even if the contents are valueless or belonged to you prior to your marriage, you will not be allowed access until the bank has received all the appropriate state and/or federal tax releases. Meeting these documentation requirements can take weeks and in some cases months. This can become a tragic problem at a crucial time. Especially if one has kept needed cash in his deposit box.

4. *Are the contents of your box insured under the bank's insurance policies?* They are almost always *not* insured. Even if your bank is one of the few that make such comprehensive insurance available to their customers, you will not be able to collect a loss should one occur. Why? Because unless you can prove to the satisfaction of the insurance company what contents were lost, you can't collect. That's what happened to many of the customers at the bank in San Francisco. They lost everything!

Proving a loss is impossible by design of the bank and its insurance company. You see, your word is not enough. Nor is that of your family. Nothing you can say or do will convince the insurance company. An interesting paradox. The bank sells you a safe deposit box and uses the advantage of confidentiality as a selling point. Then when there is a problem the bank's insurance company uses that confidentiality to deny legitimate claims!

This insurance issue is moot in most instances, as most banks have no legitimate insurance on the contents of their customers' safe deposit boxes.

In either case, insurance or no, the bank itself will not make up your loss because no loss can be proven. So don't for a moment make the mistake of thinking you will have successful civil or legal recourse with the bank.

Since I am recommending that you don't use the bank's safe deposit vault, I will give you viable alternatives that offer the safety and security your bank box does not. Assuming you are one of those who will use a bank safe deposit box no matter what I say, I will mention things for you to consider.

1. *Consider a home safe.* There are many available for under $250 that meet or exceed the fire rating a bank vault has. Proper location in the house would completely eliminate the possibility of flood damage. With the proper appraisals and a rider on your homeowners' insurance policy you will have provided the insurance protection the bank doesn't offer. At the very least, if you do experience a loss, you'll have a chance of collecting a reimbursement. That's usually not true at the bank.

A home safe would not be any stronger than a bank vault, and therefore it, too, is susceptible to a break-in. But only you will know where the safe is located, or even that you have one. An amateur won't be able to open your home safe and there is little reason to expect that a professional thief would bother. The pros would rather expend their efforts on a bank vault where hundreds of families have their valuables in one central location.

2. *If you do use a safe deposit box, make sure it's located substantially outside your market area.* The reasoning is this: A tax lien/warrant (for example) is only good if it is known where it should be served. In most cases the government agency will check only the records of banks in your hometown and immediate surrounding communities. The remoteness of your safe deposit box's location protects your assets and makes the warrant worthless.

The same reasoning holds true with a death. Your box won't be sealed if the bank is not aware that one of the owners has passed away, and that's unlikely if you're not well known in the town where you have your safe deposit box.

In both examples I am not suggesting that you circumvent the law. My alternatives are showing you how to avail yourself of your legal rights. If you have to travel a distance to use your safe deposit box it may be inconvenient, but well worth the effort.

3. *You may wish to give up your safe deposit box confidentiality rights to facilitate an insurance reimbursement in case of loss.* The only proof the bank's insurance company will accept is a safe keeping receipt signed by a bank officer. That means you will have to allow a bank official to see what you put in and take out of your safe deposit box on each visit. He or she will then have to sign to the effect of the box's contents. This receipt becomes your insurance proof.

Don't forget to ask the bank officer what insurance they do have for your safe deposit box contents. If you truly value the contents of your safe deposit box, ask for a copy of the bank's insurance policy. It would be an appropriate request.

Finally, remember this. Use caution in deciding where you place your valuables. Don't find out the hard way that a bank safe deposit box is misnamed.

Other Services

Your banker is shrewd, and uses every opportunity to exploit your finances. The two following examples may appear benign and inconsequential, but demonstrate the bank's propensity to exploit every opportunity to make huge returns on the daily transactions of a trusting and unsuspecting public.

Money Orders, Cashier's Checks, and Traveler's Checks

Typically, a money order costs the consumer approximately 50¢. A cashier's check, $2. In many areas of the country the cost for both is considerably higher. Even at the lower costs I want to prove to you that you are being abused if you use the bank for your daily financial needs.

Let's say you purchase a cashier's check worth $5,000. You are going to buy a used car, and you buy the check on Wednesday afternoon late. You close the deal on the car on Friday. The seller takes the check to his bank on Saturday. It clears back to the originating bank on the following Tuesday. That means the bank had the use of your $5,000 for six days, while at the same time charging you $2 for the check. Let's take this very simple example and perform a cost analysis.

Cashier's check for $5,000	Fee $2.00
Interest earned by bank ($5,000 × 12% ÷ 365 × 6 days)	9.86
Total earned by bank	$11.86
Minus the cost of check printing	.15
Minus the cost of handling (computer and employee costs)	.30
Net profit to the bank	$11.41

Note: The 12 percent interest rate is a fair Fed fund representational rate. It could be lower, it could be higher.

This may sound like a small amount to be concerned with, but as a consumer you have to realize that this one example would have to be expanded by millions to give an indication of how much money banks make on these services daily. Additionally, this same principle is apropos for money orders and traveler's checks. Banks make hundreds of millions of dollars by using the float in our transactions. I have no objection to that, except that they won't allow us the same privilege when we make deposits. The bank's fee for any bank check and virtually all other services is completely unjustified. How unjustified? In our example the bank expended a total of 45¢. They made $11.41. That is an interest rate return to the bank of 2,535.55 percent!

I want to repeat that figure. 2,535.55 percent! And what are banks paying on our deposits? There seems to be a disparity. As with all bank income/consumer cost comparisons, that doesn't come as much of a surprise.

Real Estate Tax Collections

Most of us pay our real estate tax bill at the local bank. We either do it in person or do it through an escrow account. We have already discussed the latter. Let's look at the former.

In exchange for providing the convenience of allowing you to pay your taxes locally, your bank once again uses your money to its benefit. The bank serves as an agent of the collector and remits those funds deposited at the bank directly to his office at predetermined times. In most large cities the taxes are remitted almost daily. In most small community banks (the largest number of commercial banks are in this category), the time the banks can use the monies collected varies from a few weeks to a few months. Let's use three weeks as representative.

Assuming a real estate tax bill of $1,500, what income is the bank able to generate with your real estate tax deposit? Remember, this is a completely different issue than our escrow discussion previously.

Taxes collected	$1,500.00
Return to bank ($1,500 × 12% ÷ 52 × 3 weeks)	10.38
Bank processing costs (computer and employee)	.50
Net to bank	$9.88

Here again, a small amount. However, to understand the impact of this principle, consider that this figure would have to be multiplied times hundreds or thousands of tax bills depending on the town or city. That means the consumer base of this community lost whatever the bank made. Further, since the bank wasn't paying any interest to the county tax collector the county lost too. The only entity that prospers here is the bank.

What return did the bank make on this "service"? In our example they had a net profit of 1,976 percent!

These are just two simple examples to help me make my point. We could dissect each and every bank "service" with the same results. Your bank will use every opportunity to take as much of your money as possible.

Because of the system, it's very hard, if not impossible, for a consumer to understand all the ramifications of any transaction. If you did understand what the real net cost to you was (remember, if the bank made money using your funds it means you were denied a return that belonged to you), you probably would never use a bank, or at the very least you would demand charges that were fair. And if that weren't possible, you would explore other options. For instance, if you knew that your local gas station was making a return of 2,000 percent on a gallon of gas would you patronize it? No, of course not. Yet that's what you're doing with your bank!

When you patronize a bank, you are dealing with an industry that is routinely guilty of what amounts to price-fixing, that is, banks don't have "gas wars" over service charges. That means the banking consumer is a captive audience. That's why the banking industry has fought so long and hard to ensure that no "nonbank" banks can enter the market. Bankers know their license to deceive consumers will be lost if real competition enters the field. For instance, aggressive nonbank banks would soon be offering money orders, cashier's checks, and traveler's checks for free, since they could settle for the use of the float to make their profit. The banking consumer must demand changes! The industry isn't going to stop overcharging on its own. There will have to be severe pressure exerted by individuals, consumer groups, and the government.

I have to say, point-blank, that I am a free market advocate. The government has no business in business. But *banks currently are not part of any competitive free market.* They have what amounts to a monopoly; that changes all the rules. Since they are allowed the benefits of a monopoly, they should assume a responsibility toward the community whose more-or-less captive business keeps that monopoly afloat. Depositors, and other consumers of bank services, have a right to be treated fairly. Service charges of any sort should be justifiable by cost analysis, or the word "service" is being misused. If the bank prospers with our money we have a right to share in that return!

Can You Trust the Trust Department?

There are many valid reasons why you might consider using a trust account. They can provide a number of important functions, from assisting in lowering your tax burden to caring for a handicapped person. But the advisability of a trust isn't the issue. The question here is, is a bank's trust department the right choice as your trustee?

Your decision should be one that gives control of your trust account to someone who is financially astute and understands your wants, needs, and expectations. In certain circumstances you have the option of being your own trustee, but, in most instances, that's not the case. For some smaller trusts a friend or relative can perform quite well as trustee, provided they are given specific instructions. However, any person, as opposed to an institution, gives rise to another problem—continuity (i.e., institutions offer longevity individuals can't). That shouldn't be forgotten.

Larger, or more complicated, trusts call for an expert. Here's where many get in trouble. They turn to their bank's trust department. Most money center banks will not even consider a trust of less than $250,000. Hometown banks usually have a cut-off of $50,000. Generally, the fees associated with a trust include a set-up charge of $X, plus approximately 1 percent of the trust's worth per year as a maintenance fee. Associated transaction expenses are occasionally assessed.

The horror stories regarding bank trust departments are numerous. The biggest problem is that, if you get locked into an irrevocable trust, the trustee, however incompetent, will continue to have working control of the trust's assets. You can go to court to fight the issue, but, unless fraud can be proven, the courts generally side with the bank and let them continue to serve as trustee. Clearly, whether you choose a bank or not, an irrevocable trust can be dangerous. There are other, more flexible, trust options available. Of course, if the trust was left to you from another, you have little choice.

Based on my experience, I can say without hesitation that many community banks have trust departments that are professionally unqualified. Too often they are supervised by someone fresh out of law school, or a long-standing bank employee who sees the trust department as a way to hide from the competition in the real world. Of course, there are exceptions.

Bigger banks present another problem. Unless your account is substantial, (close to at least $1 million) it will get little hands-on supervision. Each trust officer may have two or three hundred accounts, which means there is little time available for the smaller trusts.

So you're faced with a dilemma. The smaller bank is too often incompetent, while the larger bank is too busy to give you the management necessary for good performance. Here are some better alternatives: Trust companies, trust attorneys, and trust accountants. Regardless of who you ultimately choose, you must do your homework and have proof of their management results. Talk to others who use their services; check with professional associations. You must have complete faith in your trustee. Keep shopping until you feel comfortable.

There is another, more important, issue regarding bank trust departments. And that is honesty. Unfortunately, some trust departments use their trusts as a cheap money pool for the bank's investment purposes. Little effort is given to maximizing the return for the trust accounts. Quite the contrary. Simply stated, instead of opting for safe, higher returns they choose one of the bank's investment vehicles. And the lower the return the better. Better for the bank, not for the trust. Of course, the more money the bank's trust department can offer the bank's deposit function, the more money the bank has to invest in its lending function. And the less the bank has to pay for that money the larger their profit margin. The lending function returns high rates for the bank's bottom line, while the trust's beneficiary may only be receiving the passbook rate for their account balance(s). Many bank trust departments see their responsibility in this light. And for this "professionalism" the bank then charges a yearly trust-maintenance fee on the account.

Perhaps some are thinking this scenario can't possibly be true. Sadly, it's an easily verifiable fact. In 1984 the Comptroller of the Currency warned one hundred large U.S. banks to stop investing their trust monies in their own bank's passbook accounts. The banks in question were supposed to be investing these funds for the benefit of the trusts in safe, high return investments. Yet, they were getting the lowest return possible, the passbook rate. They were purposefully mismanaging their trusts for the benefit of the bank.

The government will do almost anything to protect banks from public scrutiny—which makes this admission from the Comptroller's Office even more alarming. The point being, when a government agency finally admits that a bank, or the banking industry, is guilty of an indiscretion, the actual scope of the problem must be so acute that the government realized it could no longer be hidden. Further, what is known publicly is only the tip of the iceberg. The actual amount of the malfeasance will never be known, but at least it was finally admitted.

Take this issue down to the smaller community banks and, because they receive even less government supervision, the problem expands. Worse yet, the problem has yet to be solved. Like so many banking/consumer issues, the government does as little as possible, and then hopes the public will forget.

Trusts are an excellent answer to many financial questions.

You shouldn't ignore their value. However, I suggest that you avail yourself of your other trust options, such as the trust companies, trust attorneys, and trust accountants I mentioned earlier. Your bank's trust department may not be competent or trustworthy. As an industry, they have already been proven guilty.

Dormant Bank Accounts

A dormant account is a bank account that has had no activity over a certain period of time. Under normal circumstances that would be as far as one would go with the subject. However, with deregulation of the financial industry, the rules have changed.

First, there is the problem of the bank acting as an agent of the state. This has always been the case and is not the bank's fault. Individual state laws dictate that financial institutions review their account files each year, and those accounts that have had no activity (interest posting does not qualify as activity) must be turned over to the state. In some states the dormant time criterion is five years, in others seven.

This presents a problem for many financial consumers. For instance, an elderly person may have forgotten an account he or she has had for decades. Estates have problems, too, as the deceased may have been the only person who knew where an account was located. Parents sometimes open an account for their children, only to forget about it as time passes. There are any number of ways an account becomes dormant and then becomes state property. These accounts amount to millions of dollars each year!

I believe that since a bank account is fiduciary in nature, the bank should be forced by law to ensure the customer is notified and the account monies returned, as opposed to remitting to the state. However, since this represents substantial state "income," most states are more concerned with their cut than in what is right.

Nevertheless, should you finally realize that you have an account that has not been used in years, and the bank says it turned the money over to the state, you can receive your money. Petition the agency that received the funds (the bank will give you its name and address) and, provided you can prove ownership (your passbook or a copy of your Social Security card is usually adequate), you will get your money back. This takes time, and the state will only remit what the bank sent it. You will not, under most state guidelines, receive any interest, even if the state has had your money ten or twenty years.

Important to this discussion is the bank's role since deregulation. Since then many of the laws that were designed to protect the consumer, no matter how inadequately, have disappeared. In the case of a dormant account, that means the bank is now allowed to take some or all the money from an account long before it has to remit to the state.

How? Numerous banks are now assessing substantial service charges on accounts that have no monthly activity. Each month the account balance is decreased by a service fee of X dollars. In most cases dormant accounts are no longer paid interest regardless of the balance size, and the bank's profit center starts eating away at the principal. This is done on both savings and checking accounts.

This is just one more reason why our country ranks last in individual savings percentages among industrialized nations. The way the banks are doing business, it doesn't pay to save. Banks are no longer satisfied with underpaying our savings interest through questionable methods of interest computation. They now want whatever principal they can get, too! The sad fact is that since most dormant accounts are relatively small and seldom remembered by the rightful owner, the bank and the state will bleed any balance dry.

Protect yourself and your estate. If you have accounts, keep them active by making a small deposit or withdrawal periodically, preferably monthly if possible. Check with your financial institution to find out what its account service charges are. If they are excessive, move to another bank. Also, make a list of all your accounts and where they are located. Keep it where your family can find it. You worked hard for the money in your bank accounts, and it belongs to you. Protect it! If you don't many banks will service-charge the account(s) until you have nothing left.

There has been another interesting development in the area of bank service charges. I mention it here because of its relationship to what banks are doing to dormant accounts. Many banks are now assessing monthly activity charges on savings accounts. Banks arrive at these fees in varying ways. Some banks have a fee for each entry during the month. Some have a fee for "over activity" as determined by the bank. Still others pay no interest at all if "interest earned" is less than $1. There is no universal example for me to give, as each bank has its own method for arriving at and assessing these fees.

This new attack on our savings is almost beyond comprehension. If we don't use a savings account they call it dormant, stop paying us interest, and start charging monthly fees. At the other end of the spectrum, if we use an account they charge us activity fees!

The actions of the industry might make you wonder why you should even bother considering a bank for your deposits. It seems that the banking consumer just can't win!

Automated Teller Machines

When automated teller machines (ATMs) were introduced, they were touted as a free convenience, providing bank customers with greater access to their money. Unfortunately, the banking industry's behind-the-scenes marketing strategy was not that altruistic. The real goal was to make ATMs a major income producer. To accomplish that customers had to be convinced that they had nothing to lose by using an ATM. First, the service was introduced at no charge. Next, dependence on the machines was created, by introducing remote facilities, 24-hour access, and most importantly, by reducing access to lobby tellers. It wasn't long before many customers were forced or persuaded to rely solely on their bank's ATM. That's when things changed.

Having integrated the system into the marketplace, the ultimate intent of the banks became apparent. Service charges were introduced. Many banks now have a $1 fee each and every time you use the machine. The greedier institutions even charge when you make a deposit! Other banks have an annual fee for your access or debit card, in addition to their per-transaction charge. Still others charge if you access your account to determine your balance.

In fairness, it has to be said that ATMs cost money to buy and operate. They shouldn't be a loss leader to the bank. The average cost per unit is $30,000, with a life span of thirty years. Using a life span/purchase price ratio, the machine costs the bank $1,000 a year. Operationally, the bank's reported computer costs per each transaction is 15¢. Should the bank have to absorb that cost? No. They are a business and have an obligation to make money. But, they are also a federally sanctioned monopoly that consistently runs to the government for help every time they have a problem. They have a free market right to make a profit, but they also have a responsibility to serve their community at a fair price. Also, since they knew from the beginning that ATMs were going to be a profit center and not a free service addition, the banks clearly deceived their customers. Needless to say, deception should not be an acceptable marketing strategy.

In actual use you have to abide by the parameters the bank has set for its machine(s). For instance, some have a with- drawal maximum of $200 per day and/or no more than five transactions per day. Most banks offer a variety of available transactions, such as making a deposit, a withdrawal, a trans- fer of funds between accounts, a loan payment, or a balance inquiry. The services offered are more than adequate and for many individuals, and for those who use a remote facility, the service can be quite convenient. But are ATM fees reasonable? Of course not! Let's review them to make the point. We'll use the $1 per transaction fee. (On balance, it needs to be stated that not all banks have these fees or fees this large, but they will. The dollar is an average I've found consistently through- out the country. You should also be aware that in the not-too- distant future you're going to look back at the dollar per trans- action charge as the good ol' days, because the banks have planned a continual rise in ATM/consumer costs.) Remem- ber, we're talking about access to *your* money, yet the bank charges you a fee. Actually, it's worse than just the fees since the bank, having use of your deposits, invests them to enhance their profits. You see how perverse a banking relationship can become when it's not dissected. It hardly seems fair that when the bank loans us money, we have to pay a fee (interest), and when we loan them money (by making deposits), we have to pay service charges.

Let's pursue the fairness aspect of ATMs. If the bank's cost is actually 15¢ per transaction (an amount I think is high on a cost analysis basis), then what is the profit on their $1 charge? Obviously they make 85¢, but what is the percentage return on their "investment"? Sad to report, it's 566.66%. At that rate it doesn't seem unfair to call the ATM fees exorbitant.

What about the cost of the equipment? Shouldn't banks be allowed to recoup that? Of course. As I said, the machine cost $30,000. A small bank records approximately 3,000 ATM transactions per month. At a dollar per transaction, it will take ten months for the machine to pay for itself. Of course, as banks are so adept at using the system to their advantage, long after the ten months have elapsed they will still be depreciating the ATM for tax purposes. Larger banks easily record more than 100,000 transactions per month. They can recoup their purchasing costs in as little as ten days, after which it's all profit. As expensive as the ATMs are initially, their long-term cost to the bank is negligible.

ATMs are acceptable as a service, but their financial reality to the consumer is not. The costs are too high—and remember, they'll go higher. Perhaps more importantly, this is yet another example that your bank cannot be trusted. ATMs were marketed first to gain acceptance, then to create dependency, then to produce profits. If banks had been fair, they would have made their intentions known immediately. That would have given us our free market right of accepting or rejecting the service based on all the facts. But, the industry decided otherwise.

There are other problems associated with ATMs. Research shows that mistakes or computer errors seldom occur with ATMs, as they truly are state of the art technology. However, on the rare occasion when something does go wrong, the customer lives a banking nightmare. The fact is, it's your word against their computer, and under those circumstances you can imagine how friendly your "friendly" banker is. Judging from my experience, if you have a difficulty at the ATM, you're going to have major problems correcting it.

It should also be noted that when you use a remote ATM you may become a target for a robbery, especially late at night. You're alone and the robber knows you'll probably have money when you leave the facility. Be careful! While it's not the bank's fault, some remote facilities are favorite targets for robberies. My complaint is that, even after certain ATM stations become an obvious problem for customers, the bank often doesn't provide round-the-clock security or close the facility. Their decision to do nothing makes them culpable in a worst-case scenario. Regardless, you should remember that an ATM's convenience may be hazardous to your health.

Additionally, if your card or access number is stolen or lost, you may have other difficulties. Read your agreement carefully. You must understand your monetary responsibility under these circumstances. You may not be willing to accept the terms the bank has outlined. Unfortunately, most people don't actually read their agreement until after a problem has arisen, and of course then it's too late.

In conclusion, if you like the convenience of ATMs, I strongly suggest that you look at the cost/benefit bottom line before deciding which bank gets your business. A few banks still allow free use of their facility (usually smaller community banks). Bank there. Or, better yet, don't use an ATM.

Assuming you can arrange your schedule to make it to the bank sometime during normal banking hours, the ATM offers less service than you can receive directly. And the lobby offers a personal touch should you have a question or problem.

When you consider the facts, in almost all circumstances an ATM is a service that you can afford to live without.

Loan Late Charges

The lending function is one of a bank's most important services. That's why I discussed lending in-depth in earlier chapters. There is, however an aspect of that service that needs to be reviewed here: loan late charges.

As you know, banks assess a late charge for loan payments that are more than ten days delinquent. The ten days are the required grace period. In most instances the late charge is $15. Bankers say that they have to charge a late fee because they lose money when a customer is tardy with their obligation. There are computer costs, personnel expenses, loss of interest revenue, etc. That sounds fair, after all; banks shouldn't have to incur a loss because a customer doesn't meet their commitment. We can all agree to that. However, I believe a closer review shows conclusively that loan late charges are excessive and unfair.

First, let's look at the charge itself. As a banker, I acknowledge the bank shouldn't have to lose money because customers fail to make their payments when they agreed to do so—but that's where other bankers and I part company. The bank should only be able to recoup its expense, it is already being paid substantial interest from the loan itself. And what are its' expenses? For example, let's review a $250 payment that is fifteen days past due.

Bank Expenses	
Computer cost	$ .25
Mailing (postage & envelope)	.32
Investment loss to bank (average loss on $250.00 for 15 days)	1.33
Employee expense (5 minutes at $6.00 per hour)	.50
Total	$2.40

In all fairness I can tell you that I am being generous in this analysis. For instance, it doesn't take five minutes to process a delinquent notice, and many staff level bookkeeping people at community banks don't make $6 per hour. That notwithstanding, let's review the bank's revenue from the late charge.

Bank's Profit

Bank fee to customer	$15.00
Less expenses	2.40
Net profit	$12.60

They spend $2.40 and make $12.60. That's a return of 525 percent! I believe *excessive* aptly describes this fee.

Now to the question of fairness.

Forget the figures above, even though they are undeniably incriminating and perhaps by themselves prove the charge is unfair. There is an even better way to judge. If the bank is willing to charge its customers for being late with their loan payments, then, in fairness, it should be willing to pay the customer $15 when they pay their payment ten days early. Reversing the bank's logic for assessing a late charge, an early payment means that the bank gets to reinvest your payment earlier than anticipated, and for that you should be compensated.

Does your bank have an early loan payment bonus? Of course not. As usual, banks have one policy for themselves and another for the customer. In each and every case, the bank profits excessively and unfairly at your expense.

When You've Been Wronged

Financial Discrimination

The Federal Equal Opportunity Act prohibits creditors from discriminating against applicants on the basis of race, color, religion, national origin, sex, marital status, age (provided the applicant has the capacity to enter into a binding contract); because all or part of the applicants' income derives from any public assistance; or because the applicant has in good faith exercised any right under the Consumer Credit Protection Act.

This is the notice that banks use on their credit applications. It could be assumed, then, that they clearly understand that financial discrimination is illegal. Logical progression dictates, therefore, that discrimination should no longer be a problem for the banking consumer.

Nothing could be further from the truth.

Banks practice financial discrimination each and every

169

business day. Remember, I was there. I speak from firsthand experience.

For the purpose of this chapter I will offer this discussion in the form of how discrimination affects the lending function. There are, of course, other areas that feel the damning results of financial discrimination, but it is felt the hardest here.

It should be obvious that the Equal Credit Opportunity Act (ECOA) was made necessary by the historical abuses of the banking industry and, as such, legal actions were required to address legitimate consumer grievances. In most cases Congress rubber-stamps whatever the bankers want. In this case the abuses were so apparent and/or racially motivated that Congress was forced by public demand to act. The banker/congressional connection was then faced with doing something without actually doing anything of tangible substance. Hence was born the ECOA, congressional cosmetics at their worst. The Act placated the consumer groups that were demanding action for banking discrimination, while giving no actual relief to those abused.

Congress then charged the Federal Trade Commission with administering ECOA compliance. The Commission has been embarrassingly weak in using its authority against financial institutions that even now continually receive complaints of discrimination. My research makes clear that the ECOA has very little, if any, merit for the consumer. It looks good. Unfortunately, that's all it does.

The proof is in the specifics. There continue to be substantial numbers of financial discrimination complaints, and yet actions against individual banks by banking agencies (the Comptroller of the Currency, the FDIC, state banking authorities, etc.) are virtually nonexistent. Actions against banks by the Federal Trade Commission are equally scarce. Congress didn't solve the financial discrimination problem; instead it gave the banks an act to hide behind.

For those of you who have never suffered financial discrimination, this chapter has little tangible meaning. Others know why I am addressing the issue. Financial discrimination can be the worst discrimination of all, for its ramifications are endless. Often, the discrimination of one bank can affect the relationship you have with another bank. If discrimination becomes a matter affecting your credit report, it can destroy a financial lifetime.

Discrimination by financial institutions and others that extend credit is easy to understand. Loan officers are only human. They are subject to imperfections and subjectivity that can adversely affect others. Good loan officers, of which there are all too few, realize their limitations and bend over backward to be reasonable toward marginal credit applications, especially if the application is from someone they do not like. Some loan officers will give the application to another officer to make the final judgment, ensuring that the consumer gets a fair answer. Unfortunately these loan officers are in the minority. Most simply fall prey to their prejudices and pass them on to the applicant, by turning the loan down out of hand.

Of course the paperwork will never reflect that discrimination. The credit denial form has a list of many reasons that can be checked to explain why you were denied, and all the officer needs to do is find one that remotely fits your circumstances. He knows no federal agency is ever going to pursue the matter; the wording of the ECOA virtually assures that. The Act calls for the loan officer to supply written notice indicating why you were denied credit. But no loan officer in his right mind will ever admit discrimination, especially in writing. Tens of millions of credit denials have been sent to applicants since the ECOA's inception. In all my research (and that includes examining the research of other consumer groups) I have never found an instance in which one of these credit denials specifically indicated discrimination. That means either banks have the most remarkable altruistic record in the history of mankind or the whole process is a sham. Logic dictates the obvious. Does the Federal Trade Commission really think that a loan officer is going to write on a denial slip: "You were denied credit because you're black [a woman, a Jew, or whatever]"?

I state without fear of being proven wrong that financial institutions routinely practice discrimination. In fairness, some discrimination has decreased, particularly racial and ethnic financial discrimination. Of course it still exists, but not like it once did. Times have changed, and banks, having been forced to finance minority businesses, forced to stop redlining, suddenly realized that those racial and ethnic groups which they had been avoiding pay their bills, too. The Civil Rights Act made its most subtle yet powerful contribution in the financial marketplace.

At this point you must be asking yourself, who else is being discriminated against? There are three less obvious groups presently being abused. I list them in descending order of volume and severity: women, the young, and the elderly.

Women are discriminated against. The starting point is that most loan officers are men. As such, they have difficulty bridging the gender gap when assessing the creditworthiness of the opposite sex. Some men don't like women in the business world. Some men don't believe women of child-bearing age will be able to make their loan payments because "what happens if she gets pregnant"? Some men don't like women to get ahead, especially ahead of them, so they deny them business credit.

Young credit applicants are usually denied credit because many banks have little foresight. That is to say, they don't want to be the first one to loan money to the untested. They want you to establish your credit rating before applying with them. The ludicrousness of that Catch-22 deserves no further comment.

Elderly applicants are often shocked to find that years of quality bank accounts with an institution count for very little when they apply for a loan. Banks don't want the hassle of collecting from the elderly if they become sick and/or disabled. Nor do they want to wait for the estate to be settled in case of death. To the point, they want your deposits. They don't want your loan business.

The fact is, although banks have shifted the focus of their discrimination, they are still in the business of denying credit to applicants based on one or more of the aspects of the ECOA. They will not be aboveboard with their actions, but when you strip away all the tinsel, they stand guilty as charged.

If you would like a pamphlet describing your rights as a financial consumer you can request a copy of "A Guide to Business Credit and the Equal Credit Opportunity Act." Write to: Publications Services, Board of Governors of the Federal Reserve System, Washington, DC 20551.

If you feel you were discriminated against in the financial marketplace, there are some positive steps you can take.

1. *Women:* consider a class-action law suit. Women's support groups may be helpful. If your application was for business credit, reapply for your loan through the Small Business Administration. Your chances for approval are fairly good here. Quite often they will find some way to be of assistance, especially if you find an SBA employee that understands what you've been through.

2. *The young:* consider a class-action law suit. Consider small claims court if your denial claim fits their parameters. Contact the Federal Trade Commission (as I said above, not much hope here, but perhaps it's worth a try). Send copies of your complaint to the appropriate banking agency (the Comptroller of the Currency if it's a national bank, the state banking agency if it's a state bank). Don't forget the FDIC.

3. *The elderly:* in addition to the above, contact your local support groups, like the American Association of Retired Persons (AARP), as they have additional information that, because of its perspective, may be helpful.

Discrimination will always be with us, as that's our curse for being human. We are less than perfect. However, that's an excuse, not an acceptable reason for allowing the practice to continue.

Have you been discriminated against? Possibly. If you haven't yet, you may be in your future. I bring the subject to your attention because it's too costly to quietly accept the results of someone else's prejudices. Common sense dictates that you know when you make a loan application whether the loan will be approved or not. You know in your heart if it's marginal or bad credit. Sometimes, on balance, the bank officer just doesn't see it your way. That happens honestly. Maybe he is too financially conservative, but that's his right.

The problem rears its ugly head when you get turned down for a request that you know should have been approved. When that happens, chances are you have been discriminated against.

I hope you will take legal action that will bring results for your personal needs. More importantly, I hope you take action that makes it so costly for banks to practice financial discrimination that they have no alternative but to stop.

Complaints and Problems

Perhaps the hardest thing to accomplish in terms of a banking relationship is resolving a problem when one arises. And I can assure you, if it hasn't happened already, at some time you probably will have a problem with your bank.

Banks are at their insensitive worst in a situation where there is an adversarial relationship. Their arrogance is based upon the fact that, through bank policy, they make all the rules, and even in those cases where the bank has made a legal error they are unafraid. Why? As stated elsewhere, government agencies charged with the responsibility of consumer bank protection are far more concerned with the welfare of the bank than with your rights. That means you're on your own.

Let's dissect the two different types of problems that can occur. First the nonlegal disagreement. For example, you receive an overdraft notice on your checking account. You don't believe your account is in fact overdrawn, and once more you are shocked at the cost of the OD service. The last you knew the OD charge was $10 and now it's $25! There are obviously some legal matters here, but none that we can immediately turn to our advantage. For the money involved we cannot consider a lawyer. Legal fees will far exceed what we might win unless we are willing to file a class-action suit against the bank's overdraft policy. In that case, a minor monetary loss on your part could turn into megabucks. However, few of us can pursue this strategy. Most will simply want to straighten out their checking account. In the process, they'd like to get the OD charges returned.

I recommend that, after double-checking to make sure this isn't your error, you go to the bank in person. Start with a staff employee—in this case, with an OD, someone in bookkeeping—and ask for his or her help. That's right, ask for help! Be as kind as you can be, because this person does not have the authority to solve your problem directly. That means he or she will be your intermediary with a supervisor. It's important, therefore, that this person likes you, and is sympathetic to your cause. If you abuse your contact person you will never get this matter resolved to your satisfaction. Look at this from the staff's side. They don't make the rules, the bank officers and board of directors do. Yet, across the counter, they take all the heat. If it were you, wouldn't you rather help someone who's polite and asks for your help as opposed to assisting someone who acts like a raving lunatic and won't let you get a word in edgewise? Bank staff-level people appreciate customers who give them the chance to be of service. I know, I was one.

But what happens when that doesn't work?

It's time to shift gears. You see, as nice as you should be to the staff, you need to be equally aggressive with supervisors, officers, and board members. They are the ones who make the policies. They are the ones who can, by themselves, solve your problem.

If you've ever had a problem that escalated to seeing a bank officer, you probably were treated to what I like to call the "banker's shuffle." You go in with a problem and get shifted from one desk to another, from one person to another. After an hour or so you're still being unceremoniously moved around, but are no closer to a resolution than you were when you walked through the front door. Once you finally get to the right person you are told, "It's bank policy," and they can't waver from the board directives. Or, and here's one of my favorites, "This is a branch and the policies are formulated at the main bank." He'd like to help, but . . .

Has this ever happened to you? It's one of the banker's favorite pastimes. It's more fun than an afternoon on the golf course!

Once you realize that you're not talking to staff people you have to get tough. Not abusive, just tough. You have to threaten to see "Mr. Higher Up," and, if need be, a board member. You have to make it clear that you're not leaving until you receive a satisfactory answer, one that's fair and equitable. If the bank made an error on your account, make someone fix it. A bank relationship is fiduciary in nature, and therefore each time a bank invades your account (through a service charge for example) it has to have a legitimate legal reason for its actions. "Bank policy" is not an acceptable legal answer! Of course, if you don't press the point it will be, but assuming you proceed, you have the law on your side if the bank is acting inappropriately.

Obviously you always have small claims court as a solution. Bankers hate small claims court more than a full-blown law suit. Why? Because in many states lawyers aren't allowed in small claims, which means it's just you against the banker. Even if the bank's lawyer is allowed you can force bank officers to testify. For what it would cost to return your OD charge it would hardly be worth it for the bank president, the bookkeeping supervisor, and other staff to waste a whole day in small claims. Besides, the bank doesn't want to be embarrassed publicly for a few dollars. The smallness of many bank problems actually works to the advantage of the aggressive bank customer. But you have to be willing to settle for nothing less than a fair solution. Once the banker realizes that you mean business he or she will find a way to help. All of a sudden that bank policy that couldn't be changed is forgotten.

Don't forget that many bankers don't like the boat to be rocked. They have good jobs at sizable salaries that they wouldn't like to lose. If the officer you're talking to realizes that you're going to bother the bank president because he or she can't solve your relatively insignificant problem, chances are that person suddenly will find a solution. And if the officer realizes you are going to the board of directors about a problem that should have been resolved in a few minutes, again, he or she will suddenly become very consumer-conscious. Aware, aggressive bank consumers can, almost without fail, solve any problem at their banks.

There are times, however, where the problem is a major

legal matter. If that's the case, find a lawyer who specializes in financial litigation. That sounds rather simple, but in fact it's very difficult. Your lawyer's financial litigation experience and expertise alone will determine the outcome of your bank law suit. I am, of course, assuming that you have a legitimate legal position.

Most of us erroneously assume that all lawyers can win a winnable case. That's not true! Our consulting firm assists attorneys throughout the country regarding financial litigation. And most of them don't have the slightest idea of what they are doing. This has nothing to do with their legal ability. It has to do with the financial industry. For instance, if your lawyer doesn't know the workings of the bank's Loan and Discount Committee, how can he know what records to demand? If he doesn't understand the varying agencies that audit and examine the bank, how will he know if your loan has been classified and what written response the bank has made to those agencies? A simple one: If your lawyer doesn't know how a check clears through the system how will he know if the bank met the obligation of a timely return? The point is, most consumers who are sued by or sue a financial institution lose. They don't lose because they were wrong. They lost in most cases because their lawyer didn't understand how the system works. They didn't know who to deposition. They didn't know what records to demand. They didn't know where to look in exam reports. The fact is, the inner workings of a bank and the banking system are not well known, which helps isolate banks and bankers from legal scrutiny and accountability.

The following examples will show how you can force positive results when you know what to do. One of our first consulting calls was from a lawyer in a southern state. His corporate client had lost $75,000 through check forgery. The corporation's bookkeeper, who would have been responsible for reporting a forgery (bank customers are responsible for reporting a forgery), was the very person committing the act. She had stolen a batch of checks and forged the maker's signature. She then took them to the bank they were drawn against and forged the name of the payee (a fictitious person). By the time the fraud was finally caught by the firm's owner it had been going on for eight months. He immediately informed the bank and the police. Mistakenly, he thought the bank would make good on its error of paying monies on a forgery. Not so. The bank's defense was a section of the law that says, in effect, that a bank is liable for the losses sustained in an account forgery for fourteen days after the statement that included the first forgery is delivered to the customer. The law indicates that the customer is equally responsible in this reporting aspect of the bank/customer relationship. In this case, the company didn't report the forgeries because the perpetrator was the person responsible for balancing the bank statement (an obvious mistake on the part of the business owner, but that's another story).

The bank was willing to settle the matter immediately for $7,000, the loss in the first statement plus an additional fourteen days' loss. The bank, of course, wanted the firm to give it a complete release from any lawsuit in return. It was adamant that it had no other responsibility.

The lawyer who called for consultation admitted that he was the firm's second lawyer. The first one had struck out completely. (He didn't, however, forget to send the firm a hefty bill, but that, too, is another story.) The new lawyer wasn't sure what he could do at this point. By this time the case was almost a year and a half old. Perhaps, he said, we should just settle.

We recommended pursuing the matter. We attacked the forgeries from many angles. First, the bank was consistently nonprofessional. We ascertained that the bank had a minimum dollar amount on check verification, which meant checks that fell below $1,000 were not checked for signature verification as the law demands (this is common practice among banks). All the checks in this case were below the minimum. Not one was verified! Furthermore, although the checks were made payable to a man's name, not one teller challenged the female bookkeeper as she cashed the checks. Not one made her endorse the checks even though she was receiving the funds. In fact, not one teller even followed the bank's own policy of check cashing.

Next, we approached the forgeries from the point of the forgery of the payee's signature. The firm was not responsible for reporting that! We also subpoenaed minutes of bank meetings when minimal dollar amounts were set for check signature verification and minutes of meetings where this matter was discussed in-house and through examiners. We never got the materials. Why? Because before they could be supplied, this very large bank, which hadn't been willing to meet its legal obligations, suddenly wanted to deal. We had been able (and there was much more involved here) to show the bank that we could prove consistent negligence on its part.

The bottom line is that this bank had been totally unresponsive for eighteen months. In less than a month, once the customer had someone who understood the system, the bank offered a settlement of 75 percent of the loss. Originally the bank was willing to see if it could win by default. When it became obvious that wasn't the case, the bank relented immediately.

The other example I want to discuss is one that may be easier to understand. We received a call from a man who had just lost $35,000 by investing in a partnership that was going under. He said he was prepared to lose the money because that was part of the cost of doing business. What was bothering him, and the reason for the call, was that he was about to lose another $35,000 because he had signed a loan guarantee for his partner, who was now going to file a personal bankruptcy. The bank therefore wanted our client to pay the guarantee to satisfy the partner's obligation. At this point I stated that the bank was, provided its documentation was correct, within its legal rights. You see, I am not always against the bank.

He said he understood that, but something seemed wrong. He said that when he and the partner had gone to the bank originally, he thought he was signing a guarantee that would allow for $35,000 to be injected into the partnership's capital. Only then did he enter the partnership. Under that understanding he signed the guarantee in the bank president's office and left, because the partner and the banker wanted to talk further. Weeks later things started to fall apart. He asked the partner why the $35,000 didn't solve the partnership's cash problem. He received no answer that made sense. My caller then went to the bank.

When he got there and looked at the checking account statements he couldn't find the $35,000 at all. It was never deposited! He went to the loan department to see if the partner had simply taken the money. He hadn't. What had happened was that this loan was a roll-over of a personal loan the partner had before my client had bought into the partnership. The loan was to pay off this over four-month-delinquent debt. This was not new money for the partnership, it was old money for the partner! Later he found out that the bank had already started legal action against the partner prior to receiving my client's guarantee.

The caller was upset, as you can well imagine. He talked to the bank's president, but was told that his guarantee was binding. There was nothing he could do but pay the debt, or the bank would take legal action against him.

At this point he didn't think a lawyer could help because he did sign the guarantee and (unfortunately, I hear this all the time) "You can't fight a bank."

I wanted the answer to a few questions. Did the bank president tell you this was a loan renewal? Did he tell you this was a personal loan of the partner's? Did he tell you that the loan was four months past due? Did he tell you that the bank had started legal proceedings against your partner? He answered no in each case.

I told the caller to go to the bank and demand to see the bank president. He should then demand a return of his guarantee and a release from the bank from all further litigation in regard to this and all matters pertaining to the partner and partnership. If the bank didn't meet the condition immediately, he was to tell the president that he intended to sue the bank for fraud. In addition to any real dollar loss he was going to sue for punitive damages. Most importantly, he was to inform the bank president that he was going to sue him personally for being a party to collusion between the bank and the partner in inducing him to sign a loan guarantee under false pretenses.

Never forget this: Personally, bankers don't care if you sue the bank. It's not their money. They have the time. The bank has the lawyers. They have the secretive nature of the business to their advantage. However, they do care when, in addition to suing the bank, you name them individually and not as a bank officer. Especially if the bank's director and officer liability insurance doesn't cover personal suits and/or actions. Then you've really got their attention, because they suddenly have something to lose too. If the case is large or messy enough, it might mean the end of their career, and they care very much about that. They aren't concerned with the bank per se, but once you give them a vested interest in your lawsuit you stand a much better chance of receiving a favorable settlement, offer, or resolution.

Additionally, I told our client, he should inform the bank president that he was not only going to file a civil suit, he was immediately going to the state's attorneys office to file criminal charges. He was also to make clear that the local media would be contacted regarding his bank problem.

I was anticipating that the bank president would collapse and give in. Going to court would, I hoped, not be necessary. It wasn't.

The next day I got a call from a very happy person, and it wasn't the bank president. The banker had complied with all our demands. My client was absolutely amazed that it had been so easy. Armed with our plan he had done in one hour what he hadn't been able to do in weeks. If he had run to a lawyer it could have taken months and years to accomplish a lot less for a lot more.

Why had this person been successful? Because he got enough information to make the bank president feel as help-less as the banker had made him feel. The banker had also been caught with his hand in the cookie jar. Had my client not been aggressive he would have lost $35,000. Many people have lost more.

The fact is, *banks break the law all the time.* Many will find that hard to believe, but it's absolutely true. Banks are run by people, and people make mistakes. Additionally, like all indus-tries, banks will have their share of dishonest workers. No more than any other industry, but no less. If you strongly believe that you've been wronged, you can't let the bank's image make you believe that you can't win a disagreement. You can! You have legal rights and remedies that you cannot afford to ignore.

Each and every day consumers lose their homes through foreclosures, farmers are removed from their property, cars are repossessed, monies are taken from checking and savings accounts—in many cases illegally. That's not to say that banks are always wrong. Quite the contrary. As a career banker I can tell you that more often than not the bank is technically right. But, even if they're right 99.9 percent of the time, a lot of innocent consumers are suffering when they shouldn't be. That's when you have to fight back!

Your Deposits Are at Risk

Bank Closings

Many people believe that thousands of banks were closed during the Great Depression. The fact is, only a portion of institutions actually failed during that time. The rest simply closed their doors and suspended operations, or took a bank "holiday." There is an important distinction between the perception and reality.

A bank holiday is what the governor of Ohio declared when the Ohio Insurance Plan (the state plan equivalent to the FDIC) collapsed, the result being that depositors' monies were withheld from their control. In this case, they could only withdraw $750 per month regardless of need.

A bank closing is when the appropriate regulatory agency believes, for whatever reason, that the institution is no longer financially viable. At that point the bank is normally sold to a bank that is sound and looking for taxpayer-subsidized bank purchases. There are numerous problems with this scenario. For instance, almost every year for the last seven years the banking industry has set a new post-Depression record for forced bank closings. Surely there will come a point when the FDIC will run out of sound banks and/or banks willing to purchase those banks that have folded. Additionally, is it prudent to have a few banks continually expanding their control over the financial marketplace? Then, too, the question has to be asked, is it wise to be encouraging reconstruction expansion based on past mistakes as opposed to market reflection? This *is* an issue, because so many of the bank closings are caused by illegal insider transactions and officer/director mismanagement and fraud. For the benefit of the consumer, banking expansion should be based on communal need as opposed to FDIC expediency and reserve limitations.

The forced merger technique only solves immediate problems, and hides from the public the fact that governmental financial agencies are, based on performance, totally incompetent. The thought that Congress is giving banks additional concessions in the marketplace is frightening when one considers the present circumstances and record.

In 1990, a bank was being closed almost daily, according to FDIC reports. Nationwide, the alternative to continued record closings is a bank holiday and capital restructuring for fully one third of all commercial banks. In either case, the consumer will lose.

Then there is the FSLIC/Savings and Loan collapse, at a time where almost one third of the savings and loan associations are insolvent by government audit. The FDIC isn't much better. Its reserves have not kept pace with the delinquent debt of the industry, which has left the country's top ten banks with a Third World lending portfolio equal to 270 percent of their capital equity. Certain banks have made billion dollar reserve-for-bad-debt transfers for this very reason, but in all these amounted to less than 1 percent of the total problem. In short, too little, too late.

Consumers must soon realize that something has to be done to protect their deposits or their money may be lost to either massive bank closings or holidays. In the first instance, money would be lost because the FDIC does not have the reserves necessary to pay back more than pennies on the dollar; in the second, the depositors would not lose a dime, they just wouldn't be able to make withdrawals, or withdrawals of any magnitude. Neither case is acceptable.

History and the present record make manifestly clear that the possibility of a banking catastrophe is highly probable. Congress has turned matters over to the bankers, the very people who have created the problem. Less and less regulation, more and more market expansion, is what the banking industry has asked for and exactly what it consistently receives. Just when the opposite should be occurring.

This need not be the case. The financial industry must, since it will not do so voluntarily, be forced to revert back to the foundation that made it great. The customer must come first, last and always. Consumers can no longer afford to be ignored by tellers, vice presidents, presidents, the board of directors, and Congress. The banks open their doors because of our money, and if, through their management choices, they close, we will be handed the bill. That's the why of this issue. Your local solid-as-a-rock bank may be just that. But it's part of a system that's in trouble. With all the interlocking relationships between major banks and their smaller correspondent banks, if and when things collapse every bank will be affected. The immediate lesson is *use caution.* Investigate your bank! It is a business, a shareholder-owned business, and as such it is subject to being closed. That means your deposits are at risk of loss.

The Federal Deposit Insurance Corporation

The Federal Deposit Insurance Corporation is an independent executive agency formed to insure deposits of all banks entitled to its insurance coverage. Its performance, until recently, has been adequate, and most consumers have come to rely on the FDIC's financial assurance that all deposits will be returned to their rightful owners regardless of the fate of the bank.

While it has long been known that the FDIC's monetary reserves were pitifully small when compared to the deposits it was insuring, it was also fairly acknowledged that those reserves were acceptable based on the number of forced bank closings coupled with the number of institutions under forced government supervision. Since the Depression, bank closings have normally been less than twenty per year. Banks on the FDIC "trouble list," the list comprised of institutions one step away from being closed, have usually been less than two hundred. In this financial climate it was of little concern that the FDIC reserve paled next to the deposits it was insuring. But times have changed.

As of May 1988, there were over fifteen hundred banks on the FDIC trouble list! That's approximately 10 percent of the entire banking community! Additionally, in 1982 forty-two banks were closed. Forty-eight in 1983. Seventy-nine in 1984. One hundred and twenty in 1985. One hundred and thirty-eight in 1986, one hundred and eighty-four in 1987, two hundred and twenty-one in 1988, and two hundred and six in 1989! The crisis is here, and it's here now. These post-Depression bank closing records can be interpreted in no other manner.

What is the cause of these alarming statistics? A thorough review reveals a pattern of government neglect and banker abuse. Each and every year since 1981 bank closings and the trouble list have been growing at record rates that should have alerted all appropriate government agencies. Yet the FDIC has done little to shore up its reserves to meet the added risk exposure.

Using the Federal Savings and Loan Insurance Corporation (FSLIC) as a model, the concern for the FDIC becomes manifestly obvious. While the specifics vary, there is a parallel. The FSLIC saw its reserves disappear and the agency collapsed.

Again, the failed Ohio insurance program also gives an indication of the road the FDIC is traveling. The Ohio plan at the time it collapsed had reserves (as compared to deposits) three times that of the FDIC, and yet it still collapsed! That's a historical reference that cannot be ignored.

Administrators of the FDIC have, as a defensive maneuver, repeatedly drawn to the public's attention the fact that the agency is backed "by the full faith and credit of the federal government." While that is philosophically soothing, it means nothing since the federal government is running yearly deficits of more than $200 billion, which is then added to the consistently escalating almost $4 trillion of national debt. Applying the lending standards of the banking industry itself indicates the government's guarantee is no longer to be seriously considered viable.

The FDIC has additional problems. In order to avoid closing large money center banks that are insolvent, which would expose the weakness of its own reserves, the FDIC has had to "nationalize," or become an owner/principal shareholder (as it did with Continental Illinois National Bank), a segment of the financial "free market." That policy will have to be employed again and again, as a staggering number of major banks have financial statements reflecting a negative net worth. That means the FDIC will be an owner of the very banks it is supposed to supervise. That conflict of interest is unacceptable since it accelerates the consumer's risk.

Depending on your point of view, the FDIC has already failed in principle, or is in the process of failing in fact. That needn't be the case. But until the banking industry starts policing its ranks, the bank closings abate and/or return to normal, the trouble list shrinks to a handful of institutions, and the FDIC reserves grow to reflect the clear and present dangers, the consumer, I am going to say it again, is at untold risk.

One final note on this aspect of the problem. First of all, consumers pay for their FDIC insurance. Banks are charged a fee for the coverage, which they pass on to the customer in the form of higher direct costs. So don't think you are getting something for nothing. You're not. Here is a more pressing consumer problem. Many people, especially the elderly, will invest only with an institution that has government deposit insurance. They strongly consider the security factor. That means that banks have a government-assisted edge in the supposedly free market. Yet that insurance may be more of a myth than reality. Why should you care? Because banks historically offer investment/savings rates below the "real market," which means bank customers are losing additional revenue possibilities based on very questionable FDIC insurance.

Additionally, since the taxpayer has been handed a $400 to $500 billion bill (which could go even higher) for the Savings and Loan/FSLIC collapse, no banker or government official can deny that when you rely on FDIC insurance you are, in effect, insuring yourself. It is completely illogical to save at an institution that pays less than market, but in the place of higher rates offers "insurance" that you will have to pay if the bank fails. Sadly, deposit insurance has become akin to a shell-game. How serious is the FDIC problem? The statistics tell the story. In 1988 the agency lost $4 billion, its first-ever yearly loss. It lost another $800 million in 1989. It lost $4 billion in 1990. More importantly, its reserves have fallen to 27¢ for every $100 it insures. Federal law recommends the FDIC have reserves, at a minimum, of $1.25 for every $100. As of this writing, its reserves are 78 percent less than minimum standards, which are, based on the S&L collapse, completely inadequate.

The truth is, most name-recognizable companies have better "insurance" through their corporate financial structures than banks do through the FDIC. The bottom line? The customer is being sold a bill-of-goods by the banks and the government. A very costly bill-of-goods that very shortly might become even more expensive.

Protecting the Banks from the Bankers

In 1929 the stock market crashed. That was the precursor to the Great Depression.

In 1932 Senate hearings concluded that large money center banks had used questionable, and possibly illegal, tactics in order to underwrite issues of stocks and bonds. Further, they determined that the banks' entry into this highly speculative investment form was in great part responsible for the crash of '29. The final result of the hearing was the Glass-Steagall Act, which prohibits commercial banks from corporate underwriting.

Glass-Steagall has stood this country well, yet is now under substantial pressure from banking lobbying groups. Their motivation is, as always, profits. Faced with the very real possibility of Third World debt losses, and the present loss of a large portion of the savings dollar to better interest rates being offered on Wall Street and in the corporate sector, banks want to enter once again the exceptionally profitable and highly volatile arena of stocks and bond underwriting.

In their presentations to Congress bankers are using quotes from such financial notables as former Federal Reserve Board chairman Paul Volcker, who wrote, "I believe legislation should be adopted promptly to give straightforward authority for bank holding companies to engage in certain underwriting activities. . . ." As hard as it is to understand and explain, even after the Wall Street "crash of '87," the new Fed chairman, Alan Greenspan, has taken the same position.

They and the bankers are wrong. Giving banks the ability to underwrite speculative issues is to risk once again the possible hazards of this procedure as manifested in 1929. The bankers of today are no more intelligent or morally superior to the bankers of that time. Therefore it is not inconceivable that the end results would be the same, or worse.

Let's remember that banks have been given a legislative monopoly based, in part, on the fact that they invest in relatively secure investment vehicles. By design they are the country's major financial provider of consumer services and as such have been allowed unprecedented concessions to enhance their profit base. Allowing their reentry to underwriting would give them an edge in an already unlevel financial playing field. The last time the banks had the best of both worlds the stock market collapsed. Glass-Steagall has for almost sixty years protected the banks from the bankers, and there is no logical reason to reverse the Act's positive results.

There are other aspects of the bankers' lobbying that need to be addressed. Underwriting by banks could be used to package bank nonperforming loans into securities that could then be sold to the unsuspecting public. That very circumstance happened in the 1920s, so it is not farfetched to fear a recurrence. There is also the possibility that the banks will start intermixing their underwriting funds with the deposits that the government is insuring. This, too, is a logical fear, since many bankers have recently been guilty of illegal insider transactions, etc. It seems likely that the extremely profitable underwriting would at some point be perverted by the industry's propensity for additional profits. Should that scenario happen we would have, in effect, the ludicrous situation of the government insuring the most highly speculative investments. This fail-safe position would encourage the banks to take even greater risks as (remember the Continental debacle) it is clear the government will not allow a major money center bank to close.

Congress should not be pressured to repeal Glass-Steagall and/or give the banks any additional rights to enter additional markets such as insurance, real estate, etc. The record of banks recently makes clear that, to protect the consumer, they need additional supervision, not less. They have made a mess of the market they are supposed to serve. They shouldn't be turned loose to spread their failures. Additionally, commercial bankers and their hometown capital, deposits, and loans don't belong on Wall Street. History taught us a valuable lesson in 1929. We can't afford to ignore it.

Foreign Debt

Foreign debt, which was once so profitable to private U.S. banks, has become a pressing national economic problem. In fact, the delinquence of much of this foreign debt may be the catalyst that ignites a nationwide banking catastrophe.

The taxpayer has been forced to subsidize the income of those banks that extend unprudent credit, as the United States is the principal contributor to the World Bank and the International Monetary Fund, where delinquent countries borrow additional monies to pay the banks their past-due interest. Without this taxpayer assistance from the private sector many major banks would be forced to close. That's as it should be.

Unsound banks, like other mismanaged businesses, should close in a true free market. However, the American Banker's Association (ABA) has lobbied long and hard for the involuntary taxpayer financial support and additional bank tax breaks that Congress has so willingly given time and time again. Is it possible that Congress and the ABA don't actually believe in a free market?

It should also be noted that shareholders of banks that have substantial delinquent foreign debt are being deluded. By allowing the banks to carry these past-due loans as "earning assets," the FDIC, the Comptroller of the Currency, and state banking agencies have become a party to the industry deception of creative bookkeeping. A bank that may give the appearance of a profitable, stable institution may not be that at all, and shareholders may see their investments subsequently lost while never understanding why. The fact is, if delinquent foreign debt were treated as the nonperforming assets (loans) they are, a number of major money center banks would be forced to close immediately.

A more important problem is the hidden cost of foreign debt. That foreign debt, which is approximately a trillion dollars, has drawn heavily from the available lending pool, which tightened money. This increased the cost of money for you, the consumer, regardless of whether your bank has foreign debtors. And this was money that could have been kept available to finance American business expansion, new car purchases, home mortgages, college educations. But because foreign debt paid the banks more profit than our market would bear, the money left the country, although it could even be argued that in doing so the banks violated the Community Reinvestment Act (CRA) of 1977. The CRA states that regulated financial institutions are required by law to demonstrate that their deposit facilities (credit as well as deposit services) serve the convenience and needs of the communities in which they are chartered to do business. The law's intent has clearly been violated.

Most financial experts agree that if the foreign debt had not left the country, loan rates, regardless of where they are at the moment, would be lowered by one to three percentage points. Let's avoid overstating the case, and use the lower figure. That means a $10,000 car loan (forty-eight-month term) costs the consumer an additional $400, due to foreign debt. A home mortgage of $100,000 (thirty-year amortization) costs an additional $79.57 per month, $954.84 per year, and $28,645.20 to complete term, due to foreign debt. And these are just two examples to make the point. Imagine the total cost for the millions of bank loans throughout the year. Imagine the total cost if we used the 3 percent figure.

As a free-market advocate I abhor government intervention. However, the facts and the bankers' misjudgments are clear. The consumer deserves protection from present and future foreign debt abuses. If the Congress cannot bring itself to act on behalf of the personal finances of the electorate it should be persuaded on the basis of the preservation of the banking industry itself.

The foreign debt crisis can no longer be ignored. Even the much heralded Mexican debt restructuring program is woefully inadequate, and is akin to offering Band-Aids and aspirin to a cancer patient.

Ignoring the problem will accomplish nothing other than adding to the ultimate cost of consumer expense.

Something Appears to Be Wrong

Most would agree that when someone excels at his or her job, that person deserves to be rewarded. That's the bottom line to the American work ethic. This pertains not only to individuals, but to industry as well. An industry's reward culminates in industry growth, which usually brings more profits. Those same profits are then passed on to shareholders and employees.

Sometimes, however, things don't seem to make sense. A case in point is the banking industry. I won't review again all the bad news regarding the financial-institution industry—the closings, the trouble list, the FDIC, the FSLIC—except to say that the statistics are truly alarming. Clearly the industry is in need of changes if we are to avoid future problems. But this section isn't concerned with that aspect of the picture. I want to draw your attention to the fact that the banking industry is playing by a different set of rules. Rules that are gouging money from your future.

I believe no one should be averse to paying for expertise in any field. This is probably more true in the area of finance than most. Herein lies the problem. Bank officers, who represent considerably less than 1 percent of the U.S. population, approximate a staggering 17 percent of those in the salary range of $150,000 to $279,999. Clearly bankers are well paid! The question is: How and why?

I can give you the *how* quite directly: *They are overcharging their bank customers.* The *why* is impossible to rationalize. Based on industry performance, bankers should be making moderate salaries at best. But business logic, shareholder fairness, and community/consumer service is not what the banking system is all about. It's designed *by* bankers *for* bankers, something the disproportionate salary figures boldly underscore.

Since deregulation, banks have raised their service charges as much as 400 percent, yet banks, even with this added revenue, continue to close at a record pace. Logically, something appears to be wrong.

I bring these facts to your attention for more than shock

value. I mention them to make it clear that you have to be careful about where you bank. You have to shop your loan requests. You should take time to ascertain what services your bank is providing, and at what cost. You and you alone must insulate your finances from those in the banking industry who are using the banking system for their own personal aggrandizement. Write your Congressional representative and express your concern—remembering, however (as discussed previously), that our representatives have a conflict of interest that causes the bankers to believe that they "own" the government; judging from the acts of Congress, perhaps they're right. That notwithstanding, banking unrest will continue and more than likely get worse.

In the meantime, think about the paradox of an industry that is reflecting post-Depression records for forced closings each and every year, while at the same time handsomely rewarding the very people causing the problem.

Again, something appears to be wrong. And since *you're paying for it,* you should be concerned.

Why You Shouldn't Buy Stock in Your Local Bank

When people think of banking they visualize large, money center banks. That's a mistake as, by institutional numbers, most are of the small, community variety. This misunderstanding of the industry's statistical makeup causes bank shareholders to feel they are protected from insider abuses by the Securities and Exchange Commission (SEC). In most instances, they're not. Of course, exchange listed stock of financial institutions is under the supervision of the SEC. However, as the majority of banks are not listed, their stock is virtually unsupervised, and their shareholders are at the mercy of bank directors, officers, and other insiders.

For those that believe their non-SEC supervised bank stock is protected by bank regulatory agencies, there is bad news. Supervisory agencies, the Comptroller of the Currency, the FDIC, the Federal Reserve and its board of governors, and state banking authorities perform no reportable investigative effort on behalf of investors. Understand the ramifications of this problem: If an insured bank is closed, depositors are paid by the FDIC, creditors are paid by asset sales, and shareholders get what's left. Usually, that's little or nothing. Yet, even with this unprotected position, and regardless of the severity of any insider offense(s), bank regulatory agencies will help isolate the offending bank and/or banker from accountability by refusing to assist in protecting your investment.

It must be noted that the majority of banks are run by honest people. But, even if your bank is in this category, an investment in an institution with unlisted stock seldom returns anything but meager dividends, as the bank wants to retain capital. With anticipated industry changes, dividends may become even smaller and more infrequent, and stock price is seldom reflective of bank profit/value due to the limitations of the local market. Then too, there are many questionable practices that, while not illegal, substantially reduce shareholder's return. At the other end of the spectrum is the bank operated by insiders that blatantly misuse their privileged position. The following reviews a few examples that expose the wide variety of problems you may encounter:

1. If you buy stock in an organizing bank, your investment will be worth considerably less than purchase price the day the bank opens, because new banks have formidable start-up costs/expenses. Once opened, it often takes years for a bank to make a monthly profit and approximately five to get back to its preopening capital condition. Normally, your stock will not earn one cent during this time, yet that's seldom explained to potential, noninsider bank investors. Founding directors, instead of risking their money, would rather use yours during this time of investment stagnation. Regrettably, after the bank starts making a reliable profit, some insiders start buying stock from shareholders that by now are tired of waiting for a return. Of course, they do so at rock-bottom prices immediately prior to when they know, because of their position, the bank has turned the corner.

2. As mentioned earlier, countless bank officers and directors are grossly overcompensated. For instance, it's not unusual for bank directors to get paid $500 to $1,000 for monthly board meetings that may last only an hour or two, and many bank officials are not above voting themselves huge raises and perks even during times when the bank is showing operational losses.

3. Numerous banks have staff that include highly paid, oftentimes unproductive, relatives of bank officers and directors.

4. A considerable percentage of banks are represented by a law firm owned by a bank director. The director acquires all the bank's legal business on a no-bid basis. In some cases the firm receives a substantial monthly retainer for performing no service. This is the reason so many banks are started by lawyers—they're not concerned with the bank per se, they want complete control of the bank's highly profitable legal work.

5. Other dubious relationships exist between banks and directors. For example, a director that owns the building the bank leases may receive rent greatly in excess of what the building would normally generate. Regardless of the offense, other directors rarely object as they want approval when it's their turn for a sweetheart deal.

6. Many bank insiders receive better loan rates, terms, and conditions than regular customers. They also receive general bank services at low or no cost.

7. Shareholders that have unlisted bank stock to sell often turn to bank staff for assistance. They want to know what the stock is selling for so they can determine what price they should expect. In too many cases they receive the wrong answer. Seldom is this fallacious information challenged, as the shareholder is not familiar with the bank's condition and/or industry standards for the sale of bank stock. Most times the transaction is aboveboard. Many times it's not, and the stock gets purchased by an insider at a below-market price.

8. Some insiders, in order to drive down the sale price of profitable bank stock so it can be purchased on-the-cheap, create a depressed market for shares. This can be done in many ways, such as withholding dividends (bank directors set dividend rates and frequency of payment). However accomplished, creating a depressed market for the bank's stock offers an excellent buying opportunity for those initiating the negative environment.

9. Some banks opt to become a one-bank-holding company. There are numerous legitimate reasons why a bank would take such a step. There is also a manipulative one. Bank insiders not concerned with their investors apply to become a one-bank-holding company because it offers them increased control of the bank. More importantly, when the bank makes the corporate conversion, directors and majority owners may have the right to demand individual minority shareholders to sell their stock to the holding company. Insiders increase their share of ownership, and therefore profits, by forcing small investors, some against their will, to relinquish their shares. A bank can use your investment for years during a time when the institution is not profitable, or as profitable as it could be, and then when it starts making substantial returns, insiders can force you out. If you refuse to be coerced and decide not to sell, your investment, because you now own stock in a defunct/closed corporation (the "former" bank), becomes worthless.

While it is impossible to name every potential insider offense, they all have one thing in common: trusting shareholders pay the bills. If bank directors and/or officers want to abuse the investment of their shareholders they can and do. That's not nearly as distressing as the fact that the transgressions are condoned by and perpetrated with the assistance of federal and state agencies that most people believe will protect their investment. Of course, shareholders can hire an attorney and pursue civil litigation, but, if regulatory agencies are truly there to protect the bank, as opposed to insiders, an aggrieved investor should be able to ask for and receive relief. It shouldn't be required to spend a fortune in legal fees to be protected from unscrupulous bankers. Hard as it is to comprehend, even if the banker is guilty of a provable felonious act you brought to the attention of banking authorities, they will not help you garner compensation.

Too many people buy stock in their local bank because they think it's a good investment. It's usually not. You could be at the mercy of bank insiders that have an agenda in direct contradiction to your financial well-being. Bankers know, because they have an unsupervised monopoly, they can get away with almost anything, including pillaging their shareholders. Granted, there are thousands of laws, regulations, and interpretive rulings that govern financial institutions, but as the record number of bank closings and the S&L bailout prove conclusively, they are seldom, if ever, enforced.

Buying stock in your local bank, an investment perceived as exceptionally secure, may be the riskiest you ever make.

Secrecy Is Destroying the System

When shareholders or depositors having a problem with a national bank writes the federal agency charged with the responsibility of supervising the national banking system, they invariably receive the following response: "We, as a matter of policy, do not disclose information that may or may not have been obtained in the course of an investigation." With this simple, but all-inclusive statement, the Comptroller of the Currency, dismisses virtually all inquiries concerning a national bank. Generally, the FDIC and state banking authorities are likewise unresponsive. Being able to hide behind this secrecy catch-all represents a major cause of the record number of bank closings.

Shareholders who, by their votes, could change directors, and therefore bank management, are given no substantive information that would allow them an educated appraisal of those in their employ. Worse yet, if shareholders or depositors know of any wrongdoing within a bank, they cannot receive confirmation of the offense or an outline of any corrective or punitive actions taken. Since the majority of bank directors and officers guilty of a malfeasance are given the opportunity to resign, as opposed to being prosecuted (to spare embarrassment to the bank), even the most outrageous abuses by bankers go unpunished. And it's all done in secret.

A depositor with a problem has the same difficulty as unsatisfied or concerned shareholders. The government will not voluntarily make available information that may help depositors with their cases, even if the bank or banker is guilty of illegalities. Regulatory agencies are so dedicated to protecting banks from public scrutiny that, not only don't they make available the results of their investigations, they won't even acknowledge whether an investigation has taken place.

Government agencies also hide behind the same secrecy that protects the banks. This allows the Comptroller the luxury of publicly presenting only those facts that are flattering to himself and his office. No one can receive any information about their national bank if the Comptroller, at his office's sole discretion, decides not to be of assistance. Based on my experience, this is the option employed almost 100 percent of the time. As you can imagine, the office takes every opportunity to use secrecy to the benefit of the suspect bank. The Comptroller is even exempt from legitimate congressional review. His office, like all agencies that supervise financial institutions, operates in a vacuum void of public scrutiny. They are even protected from most Freedom of Information Act requests.

Bankers say they need federal protection from public review and accountability to prevent a possible repeat of the Depression-era run on banks. (Although, when soliciting our deposits, they assure us that such a run can never reoccur.) By their actions, bankers and the government are indicating they don't believe we are financially educated enough to cope with the truth. The S&L crisis and the record number of bank closings would indicate their rationale for secrecy is not working.

Unfortunately, consumers and shareholders of banks are not receiving assistance from Congress on this crucial issue. The following quote from Senator Jake Garn, past chairman of the Committee on Banking, Housing and Urban Affairs, is a clear illustration of the magnitude of resistance of our legislators to full banking disclosure, "I also believe that the examination and supervisory activities conducted by the federal bank regulatory agencies are most efficiently conducted without public disclosure at every step of the process." He couldn't be more wrong.

Banks, when presented with a business loan request, will turn a corporation inside out, order audits, require personal guarantees, demand personal financial statements from corporate staff, etc., before they will make a lending decision. Yet, they fight viciously (through the ABA) to ensure that they are obligated to offer their shareholders and depositors the very minimum of cursory financial information about the bank. How can a shareholder know if management needs to be replaced if relevant information is denied? How can depositors know if they should use a specific bank if information is denied? The answer is obvious: They can't.

But the damaging effect of regulatory secrecy can become even more costly. A case in point: During congressional hearings on the Penn Square bank closing, the then staff of the Comptroller of the Currency admitted they had known of the bank's critical condition as much as two years in advance of the closing. The Comptroller's office made private recommendations to the bank and then gave the bank's staff time to take appropriate corrective actions. It would seem logical to most of us that giving the people who caused the problems time to correct them might cause more harm than good. It did. The deficiency of the bank approximately tripled during that time span. The same type of progression occurred with the savings and loan bailout—if the government had acted immediately the cost would have been approximately $5 billion instead of at least one hundred times that. History strongly suggests that time never helps in these situations. In the case of Penn Square time worked against the shareholders, depositors, and later, other banks. Banks that had large participation loans with Penn Square, like Continental Illinois National Bank, suffered huge second-level loan losses. If the government had gone public with Penn Square's problems immediately, much of the long-term damage could have been avoided.

And if this secrecy doctrine ever leads to a national banking collapse the taxpayer will be handed the bill. All of us have a monetary stake in the decisions of banks and government regulatory agencies. Yet, protection of our assets is not given priority. The government believes it is in its best interest to keep marginal banks open as long as possible, as each closing is a threat to the very system that invests each regulatory agency with its power. To further the end of self-preservation, the Comptroller and others have chosen to *perpetuate* rather than *regulate*. When a bank should be closed and the government gives it additional time to correct its deficiencies, the government is actually betting the monies of innocent investors and taxpayers. The truth is, if a bank's affairs are in such disarray that public knowledge of the facts would cause a run on the bank, the bank should be closed—immediately! In this manner shareholder, depositor, and taxpayer losses would be minimized. If the bank remains open in the hope of avoiding what looks to be inevitable, it should only be allowed to do so with the informed consent of everyone concerned.

The bottom line is whether or not bank shareholders and depositors should be informed of serious or potentially serious matters concerning their bank. To name a few matters for discussion: Are bank officers being paid excessive compensation? Are directors or officers guilty of illegal insider transactions or bank stock trading? Has the bank experienced any defalcations or embezzlements? Is bank management qualified and performing up to industry standards? Are bank loan losses in excess of the norm of this bank's peer group? Is the bank on the FDIC's trouble list? Is the bank under any cease-and-desist order(s)? Is the bank about to be closed? The government will not offer this information even upon direct inquiry; it has failed to (or refuses to) realize that secrecy does nothing but protect the guilty or unprofessional banker.

Bankers are members of the most exclusive and secret club in America. Sadly, the public is denied access even though we're the ones that pay all the dues.

Banking's Dangerous Capital Flaw

Banks are a unique business. What other corporate entity makes the customer pay for the on-the-shelf product? Compare a bank to any retail store. Do the patrons of the store have to pay for the shelf stock before they purchase the same stock at the retail level? Of course not, but that's what bank customers do. They deposit money (stock the shelves) so they can purchase the same product (money). Even bankers would have to admit they have the best of both worlds. Retail stores have a 100 percent investment before they open their doors. Banks don't. They have little investment. Typically a bank's capital to asset ratio is 7 percent—unfortunately, many banks are even below this minuscule percentage, and yet they are big business. How? By using other people's money. Banks are nothing more than middlemen. They are, judging by every generally accepted business practice and ratio, grossly undercapitalized. Therefore, because of their capital structure and resource allocation, even the most healthy are subject to immediate collapse.

Banks have in cash reserves only a small portion of the bank's total deposits. Even totaling their investments that might be termed liquid—immediately salable loans, bonds, etc.—doesn't help. Why the small liquidity? The industry is designed to have most of its investments in loans—consumer loans, car loans, mortgages, etc.—that cannot be turned into cash under normal circumstances. Most banks are at least 75 percent loaned out, so they have only a small portion of assets that might be turned into cash.

Consequently, it doesn't matter how strong or profitable a

bank is, the fact remains, if a large enough number of deposi-tors on any given day ask for their money, the bank cannot comply. The bank, in effect, would be closed. Without con-sumer confidence any bank can be closed, the strength of their financial statement notwithstanding. This precarious capital flaw was designed by greedy bankers. And they perpetuate it by lobbying strenuously every time someone suggests subs-tantially raising the banking industry's capital structure, or adding regulations that would better protect the consumer's money and rights. They want limited risk with their capital. Our deposits are another matter. The point is, each individual bank, and therefore the industry as a whole, is exceptionally fragile. Does this give credibility to the banker's argument that they need a veil of secrecy to protect against the destruction of consumer confidence? Quite the contrary. As the system is so fragile, again, by the design of bankers, shareholders and depositors are entitled to know the true status of their bank. How else can they protect their investment or deposits?

This subject wasn't critical when the banking system was stable, but current events make it apparent that it no longer is. Banking's state of looming crisis mandates an understand-ing of its capital deficiency. The inner workings of the busi-ness stipulate that a Depression-type problem is possible even under the best of circumstances. In today's climate it becomes all too conceivable.

Deregulation

Throughout the book I have indicated my concerns regarding deregulation: It's time to review the subject in-depth.

Deregulation, approved by Congress at the insistence of major money-center banks, was touted as the Second Coming for bank consumers. Now, for the first time, depositors would receive interest on their checking account balances, and there would be free market competition for our savings dollar. It was anticipated that competition would help increase savings rates across the board. Competition was also supposed to free up money for housing starts, mortgages, small business lending, etc. It was with this consumer benefit thrust that banks championed bank deregulation.

Big banks spent time and money convincing Congress that deregulation was in the best interest of those the legislators represented. All banks, once deregulation became a reality, spent additional time and money convincing the public that their needs could be better served by allowing the market to dictate their cost of money. To be fair, deregulation did hold promise, yet there were many of us in the industry who had grave reservations.

Immediately, bankers' motives were suspect, despite their seemingly altruistic insistence on the benefits to the consumer. The timing of deregulation, which was born at a time when industry excesses were indicating the industry was in jeopardy, makes clear the bankers' true intentions. We've already discussed the record number of bank closings. Unfortunately, this was the fertile field that spawned deregulation. It should have been apparent that an industry that couldn't function in a highly regulated environment would not fare any better left to its own devices. Banks had decided to pass the burden of being responsible for their own performance and destiny to the consumer, and deregulation was the perfect vehicle to achieve that end.

Over and above the industry concerns, there were other more important consumer considerations. Notwithstanding the promise of deregulation, certain facts became obvious. While it is true that checking account balances could now receive interest, it is also true that added service charges more than off-set the income. In fact, most consumers are paying more for services than ever before. Despite the moral imperative of their banking charters, bankers used deregulation to, in many cases, price their services out of the reach of many of the consumers they are supposed to serve. Bankers believe higher costs to fewer customers is a more profitable combination than fair costs to many customers.

It should have occurred to Congress that they were being sold a bill of goods, as common sense dictates the average family owes more than they have saved. Therefore, while competitive interest rates in the savings arena would have a positive effect on a few, the associated rise in lending interest rates would have a negative affect on many. And this ignores the increase in service charges. The net effect to the banks has been record loan and service charge profits; the net effect to the consumer has been less, and more costly, service. I keep hammering on this point because it's so important.

Further, it has to be noted that deregulation has offered the banking industry the opportunity to replace or repackage existing services that were historically beneficial to the consumer. The best example is ARM's, which we reviewed earlier. The bottom line here is: Banks advocated deregulation as a consumer benefit, and then, once approved by a malleable, willing Congress, repackaged as many services as possible to isolate the industry from any exposure deregulated free market forces might bring. They effectively flipped a coin and called heads—and tails.

There are two questions that need to be addressed. First, can the banking industry survive deregulation? The answer is yes, provided that deregulation is rethought and relegislated. Most urgent of all is the need to impose capital requirements substantially above those presently in force. No other business, as an industry, could exist with the minuscule capital that banks are allowed to operate on. Let's not forget what minimum capital requirements did to the S&Ls. Capital is important because of the fiduciary nature of the business and the growing concern that the industry may have problems that cannot be solved without extensive damage to innocent depositors, stockholders, and taxpayers.

Second, what is the future effect of deregulation on the consumer? The answer to that is in the hands of Congress, which is not a comforting thought. Will Congress force banks to, once again, service the entire community at a fair price, and, for example, provide a safety net for the elderly and less affluent who can no longer afford basic banking services needed to exist in today's economy? Will Congress intercede before ARM's trigger a record-setting rash of home foreclosures? And, of course, there are many other such considerations.

It appears that the system will not change, and bankers will continue to have their way with Congress, which is why you must protect your family finances and investigate your bank.

(*Author's note:* I have mentioned before that I am a free market advocate. I mention it again so, regardless of the gist of this section, you don't misunderstand my intentions. I believe banks should be part of the free market. However, deregulation didn't accomplish that goal, it simply made the banking industry an unregulated monopoly.)

Investigate Your Bank

The picture I have been painting in the last few sections is so gloomy you might think I see another crash around the corner. While that's clearly possible, at this point it's not imminent. However, because of the uncertainty of the moment, I do believe these are times when you should investigate your bank very carefully. By refusing to bank with an institution that has noncompetitive practices and that doesn't serve the community, you will not only help yourself, but the economy as well.

How does the average consumer check on a bank? It's simple. First, you should check the local newspaper every quarter, as banks are required to publish a *call report*. Look in the capital section, and see if capital is enlarging every quarter. If so, the bank is showing a profit, which is a sign of stability. Also, check the bank's loan loss reserve. If it is increasing along with capital, it probably means the bank is not charging off too many loans (a sign of good asset management). The bank's deposits should be growing in a steady manner. No growth or extremely rapid growth are both normally signs of future difficulties.

For a more detailed review of the bank's condition write to the FDIC, Disclosure Section, 1776 F Street NW, Washington, DC 20429. Give them your bank's name and address, and tell them what quarter's report you want. The report you will receive is more than adequate to determine if your bank is having trouble, especially when you look in the loan section.

An even more in-depth report (which includes industry standards and comparisons) of your bank or savings and loan association can be obtained by contacting VERIBANC, Inc., P.O. Box 2963, Woburn, MA 01888. Phone: 1-800-44Banks. There is a charge for this service; how much depends on what type of report you want. VERIBANC's brochure, which is free, outlines its fee schedule.

I cannot stress enough that you must make an effort to insure your deposits. The best way to accomplish that is to make sure you are depositing with an institution that deserves your trust. Don't depend on the FDIC. Don't depend on the largeness of your bank for security, for as VERIBANC reports, a number of the nation's largest institutions are among the most unsafe.

There are banks in every state that are poised to close.

There are very small community banks that are in the same pitiful condition as some of the banking giants. Protect yourself! Invest time and effort before you deposit a dime. Your bank's stability, or lack of it, must be known to you, now more than ever.

Conclusion

At the start of this book I challenged you to reserve judgment on my statement that your bank is your financial enemy. It's time for your answer. I believe that after reading this book you will conclude that I am right in my assessment.

Frankly, because I care so much about the consumer, I wish I was wrong. I take no pride in realizing that a system I believe in strongly, the banking system, is abusing the very people who allow the system to function in the first place.

Perhaps the system is just too big to realize that every customer is important, and by virtue of the fact that someone is a "customer," that person deserves respect and fair consideration. You and I know banks don't believe that. Their actions speak louder than their words and advertisements.

Sadly I report that things will get worse. Deregulation, the worst thing that has happened to the bank consumer in decades, has exacerbated the problem. Instead of allowing real competition in the marketplace, deregulation is offering the consumer fewer and more costly choices. The big banks are buying up the little banks. And the bigger a bank gets the less responsive it is to the needs of the individual. Look at the record. Deregulation has given the consumer what, exactly? I'll tell you: Less service at four times the price.

Bankers and the Congress want bigger and bigger money center banks. They believe, judging by their actions, that there is no place for the community bank, and that fewer and fewer banks and bankers should control more and more of the nation's resources. They couldn't be more wrong.

Worse yet, the conflict of interest the government has in relationship to the banking industry has become increasingly obvious. That means the consumer is at ever-expanding risk. Remember, banks are closing at record rates. The FDIC trouble list is huge! Why should we, the banking consumers, trust these people with our deposits? They can't handle their own business, why should we entrust them with ours? And yet Congress is consistently giving the banks more and more monopolistic concessions: Better tax breaks; new markets, such as underwriting, insurance, real estate; and isolation from corporate competition. It seems that the more banks mismanage our deposits, the better things get—for them, not for us. We seem to be paying more for less each and every day.

Bankers know that they are completely isolated from true free market forces. Clearly it pays banks to take big risks with our money: If the bank is big enough the government won't let it fail like other businesses are forced to do. That means a bank can abuse its customer base without fear of the ultimate bottom-line retribution, bankruptcy.

The fact is, banks are getting this country into deep trouble. They have a stranglehold on the economy. They have a stranglehold on the government. That means they have a stranglehold on us.

Yet, as important as that is, that's not the thrust of my

message. The immediately important thing is that your bank is an adversary, and should be treated as such. Banks need us more than we need them, but they don't know that. So we have to understand how they play the game. They will take as much of your money as you allow them to take.

Because of that, you must explore all your options. Don't just blindly follow what the banker says. The truth is, in a technical sense, most bankers aren't that good at their job. Want proof? Go in and ask your banker to explain exactly how they compute the Rule of 78s on an installment loan, or the compound savings interest on day-of-deposit-to-day-of-withdrawal, compounded and paid daily. Don't settle for haphazard ramblings. Ask for a specific, documented answer. Chances are he or she won't be able to give you one, because he or she doesn't know. Bankers know how to overcharge you for services, but beyond that their knowledge is severely limited.

A thorough review of any banking relationship brings one to the conclusion that either the bank will use you or you'll use it. It's up to you. In those instances where you can't get the banking service you need at the price you want, remember your other options. You don't *have* to deal with banks; you should only use them when it's profitable for you to do so.

It's amazing to me that people who will travel across town to save 3¢ on a gallon of gas, or 5¢ on a can of corn, don't bother to shop for a bank. Actually, you should shop for each banking service, not just "a bank." A bank can take more money from you in a minute than the grocery store or gas station could take in a lifetime, and yet few people bother to exercise consumer caution when dealing with a financial institution.

How do banks get away with it? They spend time, money, and effort ensuring their position. They have lobbied long and hard for the legislative right to financially abuse their customers. They spend time, money, and effort to create an image and atmosphere that intimidates the consumer. They also spend time, money, and effort ensuring that no others can enter their monopoly and create true competition for our business.

There isn't a banker in the world who can justify the charges a bank assesses for an overdraft. There isn't a banker in the world who can refute the bank officer illegal-transactions scandal that has adversely effected so many institutions. There isn't a banker in the world who can dispute that taxpayers are subsidizing billion-dollar banks through the tax system and outright grants to the World Bank and the International Monetary Fund. There isn't a banker in the world who can deny that the FDIC reserves are pitiful in these times of record bank closings. There isn't a banker in the world who can justify making families give multibillion dollar banks an interest-free loan by putting unreasonable hold times on their deposits. There isn't a banker in the world who can justify the deception of varying methods of interest computation on our loans and savings.

The fact of the matter is, bankers know they are your financial enemy. They just hope you never realize it.

Your Bank's Report Card

Although there are, of course, numerous other considerations, this quiz will help you decide if your bank is capable of meeting your financial needs.

Answer each of the following questions with a yes or no. Keep track of your score.

Checking

Does your bank:

1. Offer truly free checking?
2. Call you when your account is overdrawn?
3. Pay, as opposed to return, your occasional small overdraft?
4. Give you immediate usable credit on all your deposit items?
5. Waive the OD charge for your occasional overdraft?

6. Pay your postage if you bank by mail?
7. Return your cancelled checks with your monthly statement?
8. Offer free account balancing when you're having difficulty balancing your monthly statement?
9. Verify all your checks for forged signatures, as opposed to having a cutoff where there's no verification for checks below a certain amount (usually $1,000)?
10. Process stop-payment orders within minutes to protect your deposits?
11. Offer on-line computer services, so your account is always accurate and immediately current?
12. Have no charge for uncollected funds returns?

Savings

Does your bank:

13. Pay day-of-deposit-to-day-of-withdrawal interest, compounded and paid daily, on all its interest-bearing accounts?
14. Have a wide variety of savings plans and options?
15. Offer savings accounts that are activity- and service-charge free?
16. Offer market competitive interest rates on all its savings accounts?

Loans

Does your bank:

17. Offer mortgage closing costs based on a flat fee as opposed to a percentage assessment?
18. Offer and recommend consumer loans without credit life and disability insurance?

19. Offer single payment, simple interest consumer loans in place of installment loans?

20. Work with customers who have delinquent credit obligations, especially those having difficulties due to circumstances beyond their control?

21. Allow creditworthy consumers to borrow unsecured?

22. Have loan department specialists—consumer loan officers, business loan officers, SBA loan officers?

23. Have free personal credit checks for loan applications?

24. Waive loan application fees of all kinds?

25. Offer participation loans for applications over the bank's legal lending limit?

26. Offer loans for any worthwhile purpose?

27. Have credit card rates competitive with present consumer loan rates (if the bank offers a credit card)?

28. Have a competitive yearly fee for its credit card? No monthly activity charge? Waive all interest charges if the balance is paid in full each month?

29. Offer flexible loan terms for creditworthy but "unusual" loan requests?

30. Offer you lower interest rates because of your exemplary payment record?

31. Have no penalty charges for early loan repayments?

32. Pay market-competitive interest on its escrow accounts?

Miscellaneous

Does your bank:

33. Have insurance on the contents of your bank safe deposit box?

34. Treat you with respect and courtesy regardless of the size of your account balance?

35. Offer free assistance for all your account needs (for in-

stance, no charge for calling to check your account balance)?

36. Offer basic bank services twenty-four hours per day?
37. Make available, at all offices and branches, current call report statements indicating the bank's stability and financial strength?
38. Have a staff that truly can be called knowledgeable?
39. Have local ownership?
40. Offer a variety of free financial educational information to interested bank consumers?
41. Have directors, officers, and staff who are active in community affairs?
42. Have a qualified, result oriented trust department?
43. Offer reasonably priced brokerage services on premise?
44. Have convenient lobby hours six days a week?
45. Apologize when it makes an error on your account?
46. Offer free or low-cost money orders, cashier's checks, traveler's checks, and certified checks?
47. Have a drive-in facility and/or convenient locations?
48. Have a representational staff based on race, creed, color, national origin, and sex?
49. Invest in the community, as opposed to having large balances of government securities, Third World debt, other foreign debt, etc.?
50. Above all, make you feel that they want and respect your business?

If you answered "no" ten or more times on this questionnaire, it's time seriously to question the advisability of continuing your present banking relationship.

Directory

The following is a directory to assist you in resolving any dispute with your bank that cannot be resolved at the local level. Government agencies do as little as possible to assist a financial consumer, however, if you're aggressive, dedicated, and tenacious you can produce results.

Of course I recommend that your first attempt in resolving any bank difficulty be made directly with a bank officer. If that fails, ask to see the president. If that fails, contact the board of directors. Lastly, consider small claims court, if appropriate. If you're still unsuccessful it's time to take more potent measures. This directory is a means to that end.

1. The White House
   1600 Pennsylvania Ave.
   Washington, DC 20006
   (202) 456-1414

2. Your Senator
   The Senate
   Capitol Building
   Washington, DC 20001
   (202) 224-3121
3. Your Congressman
   The House of Representatives
   Capitol Building
   Washington, DC 20001
   (202) 224-3121
4. For problems pertaining to your mortgage loan, contact:
   The Department of Housing & Urban Development
   451 7th St. SW
   Washington, DC 20024
   (202) 755-6420
5. If you feel your financial institution has broken any law
   as it pertains to your account(s), contact:
   The Department of Justice
   10th St. & Constitution Ave. NW
   Washington, DC 20530
   (202) 633-2000
6. If your bank has discriminated against you and/or you
   have been denied credit due to race, color, national origin,
   sex, marital status, or age, contact:
   The Department of Justice
   Civil Rights Division
   10th St. & Constitution Ave. NW
   Washington, DC 20530
   (202) 633-2151
7. If you are a victim of a fraud perpetrated by a financial
   institution, contact:
   The Department of Justice
   Fraud Hot Line

10 St. & Constitution Ave. NW
Washington, DC 20530
(202) 633-3365

8. For all problems and/or complaints involving a national
   bank (those banks with the word "National" in their title),
   contact:
   Comptroller of the Currency
   Administrator of National Banks
   409 L'Enfant Plaza East SW
   Washington, DC 20219
   (202) 447-1750

9. If any problem with your bank effects your taxes, contact:
   Internal Revenue Service
   1111 Constitution Ave. NW
   Washington, DC 20002-6433
   (202) 566-4743

10. For any problem with a national or state bank, contact:
    The Senate
    Banking, Housing & Urban Affairs
    534 Dirksen Bldg.
    Washington, DC 20510
    (202) 224-7391

11. For any problem with a national or state bank, contact:
    The House of Representatives
    Banking, Finance & Urban Affairs
    2129 Rayburn Bldg.
    Washington, DC 20515
    (202) 225-4247

12. For any problem with a national or state bank, contact:
    Board of Governors of the Federal Reserve
    Federal Reserve Bldg.
    Washington, DC 20551
    (202) 452-3000

13. For any problem with a bank that offers FDIC insurance, contact:
Federal Deposit Insurance Corp.
550 17th St. NW
Washington, DC 20006-4801
(202) 389-4221

14. For any problem regarding a savings and loan association, contact:
Office of Thrift Supervision
1700 G St. NW
Washington, DC 20552
(202) 906-6000
or:
Savings Association Insurance Fund (SAIF)
550 17th St. NW
Washington, DC 20429
(202) 898-3542

15. For any problem with a bank that is a member of the Federal Reserve System, contact:
Federal Reserve System
20th St. & Constitution Ave. NW
Washington, DC 20551-0999
(202) 452-3684

16. For any problem with your bank stock, and/or any brokerage transaction your bank may have processed, contact:
Securities & Exchange Commission
450 5th St. NW
Washington, DC 20001-2719
(202) 272-2650

17. For problems in acquiring a Small Business Administration (SBA) guarantee from your bank, and/or any problems with your SBA loan, contact:

Small Business Administration
1441 L St. NW
Washington, DC 20005-3524
(202) 653-6823

18. For your state banking authority's address and phone number, call local information. Normally this agency is located at the state capital. You should contact it for all problems regarding banks that do not have the word "National" in their title.

19. For information and advice regarding other appropriate federal agencies that may be able to offer consumer aid, call local information and ask for your nearest Federal Information Center. They will give you assistance and direction.

20. I believe your best government assistance can be garnered from your congressman, who will probably be more sensitive to the importance of an individual voter's needs. For the fastest and most productive response contact the representative's local district office. The address and number is listed in the phone book. If possible, make a personal visit to present your grievance.

21. If you need a lawyer's assistance, and you don't presently retain an attorney, contact your local American Bar Association's lawyer referral service and relate the details of your problem. That service will recommend an attorney specializing in the legal requirements of your case. The number is available through telephone information.

22. Don't forget your local state agencies, such as the state's Attorney's Office, the state Justice Department, the Office of Consumer Fraud, etc. All their numbers are either in the phone book or are available through directory information.

Answers to Questions Your Banker Hoped You'd Never Ask

Loans

Q: What should I do if I can't make my loan payment on time?

A: You should never allow a loan payment, especially a house payment, to become past-due. The moment you realize that you will be late with a payment you should contact the bank, preferably in person. Explain your difficulty and make sure the loan officer understands that you don't want to damage your credit rating. In most cases they will arrange a new payment schedule that will allow you to make your payment on time by moving the due date back to a time when that will be possible. This helps the bank too, as it removes a past-due loan from their delinquent list.

If you have severe problems you should ask for a loan extension of a number of months. Of course, there is a charge for this service. But it will be money well spent, as whether you actually can pay your payment on time or not, you can't afford to let it become delinquent.

Q: What happens if the bank forecloses on my house?

A: First, the bank must go to court to prove that you are delinquent. Once that's established the court will give them the right to sell the house to the highest bidder. The proceeds are applied to the remaining mortgage balance. If they sell the home for more than you owe, you are given the difference. If it's sold for less than you owe, they may sue to collect the deficiency.

A word of caution. Some banks make little effort to sell a foreclosed property for anything more than the approximate mortgage balance, even if there is a substantial equity available. Even though they are obligated to try and obtain a fair market value, sweetheart deals on property foreclosures are far too common. If you are involved in a foreclosure, follow the sale closely. Find out who bought the property, and what if any relationship they have to the bank and/or its staff. If there is a connection, or if the property was sold far below what you know it was worth, you may wish to file appropriate complaints and a law suit.

Q: If the bank forecloses on my house is there anything I can do before it's sold?

A: Your first line of attack is to try and renegotiate your mortgage with the bank. If that's not possible you can bring it up-to-date by paying the late payments prior to the foreclosure sale. That may not be possible, but it is an option.

Of course, you always have, assuming you're employed, a Chapter 13 bankruptcy. This stops your creditors from harassing you, while at the same time setting a more realistic extended payment schedule. Additionally, even after a foreclosure has started many states allow the homeowner a one-year redemption period. In some instances that applies even after the foreclosure sale.

Lastly, the moment you start having problems meeting your mortgage obligation, see a lawyer. If you can't afford one contact Legal Aid (they are in the phone book).

Q: Can a bank repossess my car if I've missed only one payment?

A: Technically, yes. Although most banks, under most circumstances, wouldn't.

Many states now have very favorable consumer protection laws regarding car repossessions. So, regardless of the circumstances, don't automatically assume the bank is within its rights. If your car is missing report it stolen to the police. Later, if you find it was repossessed, you may wish to contact your state's banking authority to see if the bank met its legal obligations. If you believe you have been wronged, call your lawyer.

A helpful hint: Never, unless you are voluntarily giving the bank the car, sign the back of the title as Seller. This is true even if the bank officer tells you you have to. Doing so all but assures waiving of any and all rights you may have had.

Q: My small business loan was tied to the prime interest rate. But, when I checked my monthly bills it looks like they were in excess of what I should have been charged. Is there anything I can do?

A: This is a very complicated subject. You need a lawyer that specializes in financial litigation, especially if the amount in question is substantial.

What confuses many is that the mechanics of fixing prime can be extremely arbitrary from bank to bank. The universal, industry-wide prime may be at X percent, while your bank's lending prime, as it pertains to your loan, may be at the universal prime plus. Consequently, whenever the prime is used in a loan you must ascertain, before you sign anything, exactly how it is calculated and how it will be applied. Assume nothing. Get it in writing. On a large commercial loan a misunderstanding of your bank's application of prime may cost you thousands.

Q: I was delinquent with a commercial note payment. The bank went into my personal checking account and took all the money it needed to pay-off the loan. Can they do that?

A: While there might be some extenuating circumstances, the bank was probably within its rights. Most people are not aware that a bank has the right of setoff, which allows it to take money from any associated account in their institution if the customer owes them a delinquent obligation.

A bank's right of setoff can cause great difficulty, as it can spread a financial crisis. You may wish to remember this if and when you start to have a loan problem.

Q: How far can a bank go when collecting a past-due loan?

A: As outlined in the Fair Debt Collections Practices Act, a bank cannot "harrass, oppress, or abuse any person in connection with the collection of a debt."

If you feel the bank has exceeded its authority, you should start making a diary of all the collection events from that date forward. If you decide to sue the bank and/or they take you to court, a complete record will help protect your rights.

Additionally, if you even *feel* harrassed you should contact the Federal Trade Commission in Washington, and every and all banking agencies. When you know you're being harrassed you should acquire legal assistance.

Q: My bank misreported my loan account to the credit bureau. In effect they doubled the amount I actually owed—it reported $80,000, when the balance was only $40,000. My guess is this happened because my original loan of $40,000 was renewed once. Consequently, I was denied a loan at a different bank because I was "overextended." Is there anything I can do?

A: Anyone that reports credit must do so accurately under the guidelines of the Fair Credit Reporting Act. Any willful or negligent noncompliance can cause the bank civil liability for actual and punitive damages. Contact your attorney.

Q: What laws protect borrowers?

A: The Equal Opportunity Act, Fair Credit Reporting Act, Electronic Funds Transfer Act, Truth-in-Lending Act, Fair Credit Reporting Act, and the Fair Debt Collection Practices Act. For free copies of these important acts, write: Federal Reserve Board, Consumer Affairs Division, 20th St. & Constitution Ave. N.W., Washington, DC 20551.

For free copies of additional consumer protections, write: Federal Trade Commission, Pennsylvania Ave. at 6th St. N.W., Washington, DC 20580.

Of course, depending on the nature of a borrower's problem, there may be other important considerations you should explore with legal counsel.

Q: Is home mortgage insurance a good buy?

A: Mortgage insurance is a decreasing term policy that pays the bank the remaining loan balance if the insured dies. I don't recommend these policies, as, like credit life insurance, the funds are used to pay the bank. A much better idea is buying, from your insurance agent, a straight decreasing term policy in an amount equal to your mortgage. This accomplishes the same thing as mortgage insurance, but gives your family important flexibility to use the money as they see fit.

Q: How long do I have to pay for PMI insurance on my home?

A: PMI (Private Mortgage Insurance) is required by many lenders when the borrower doesn't have the required purchase downpayment. For example, if the bank requires 30 percent down and you only have 5 percent, your PMI will insure the 25 percent differential. The bank, therefore, is only exposed for the 70 percent that meets their lending requirements.

The problem that most experience with PMI is that it isn't cancelled by the bank or the insurance company once your mortgage meets the original downpayment criterion. You qualify for cancellation because, in most cases, a home appreciates in value. Additionally, you are paying down the mortgage balance. Perhaps you made substantial home improvements that add to the home's value. There are many ways you can meet the bank's requirement at a later date.

Once you feel you have qualified you should contact the bank and request waiver of your PMI insurance. There is no reason for you to pay for insurance that has ceased to have value. You will save years of expense if you'll take the initiative.

Q: Does it pay to borrow using a TCD as collateral?

A: In most instances, yes. The bank will normally charge you two to four percentage points over the interest rate they are paying you for the certificate. Depending on the term of the TCD and the timing of your lending needs, this will cost much less than the early withdrawal penalty.

In addition, I recommend the following: When investing in

a TCD use the minimum deposit requirement regardless of the size of your deposit. For example, if you have $10,000 and the minimum requirement for that certificate term is a deposit of $1,000, have the bank make out ten TCD's for $1,000 each as opposed to one for $10,000. That way, if you must withdraw money for an emergency, you will only be penalized for the money you need to withdraw instead of the entire $10,000.

Q: Is there anything that I can do to cut the high fees assessed with most loan applications?

A: As outlined throughout the book, you should always attempt to negotiate away any and all fees.

You should also consider any additional creative things you can do to cut expenses. For instance, many banks have a $50 to $75 credit check fee on mortgage applications. Did you know that you can go to the credit bureau and purchase your up-to-date report for approximately $10 or less? Take the report to the bank, hand it in with your application, and save the difference.

If, after receiving your report, the bank still wants to charge you their credit check fee, find another bank.

Checking and Savings

Q: On my bank statement I noticed the following: "This statement is presumed correct unless you notify the bank within thirty days." What happens if I find a bank error after that time has elapsed?

A: Regardless of the bank's disclaimer they cannot profit from their error. They would have to repay your money and any interest you may have lost.

Q: What are the rules regarding a stop payment?

A: You may give a stop payment over the phone, but it is only valid for ten days unless you follow it up with written verification. That notice obligates the bank for another six months. If you want to extend that period you have to sign another stop payment prior to the six months elapsing.

If a bank pays a check that's been correctly stopped, assuming it has had a reasonable amount of time to disseminate the stop payment information to its staff, it must refund your money in total. Of course, if the check was cashed prior to your stop payment order the bank is relieved of any responsibility.

A word of caution. A stop payment on a large check can, if the bank makes a mistake, represent a large loss, especially to a smaller bank. If the loss is big enough the bank may try not living up to its obligation and/or give you a hard time hoping you don't know the law. If you feel there is anything wrong in their response see a lawyer immediately.

Q: What happens if someone steals my checks and forges my signature?

A: This is a very complicated matter as there are many possible outcomes. Each case would have to be dissected completely before arriving at an answer.

In most instances a customer is obligated to contact the bank within fourteen days of discovering a forgery. At that point, since the bank is obligated to know the signatures of its depositors, it must refund your money.

Q: I deposited a sizable check. Five weeks later it was returned "Account Closed," and charged against my account. The bank the check was drawn against refuses to pay me. What can I do?

A: You are probably a victim of a late return. While the laws pertaining to negotiable instruments are voluminous, in general it's conceded that a bank has until midnight of the banking day following the banking day of receipt to return the check or it's paid. Your bank should help you collect your money, but don't count on it. Banks like to stick together in case they need a favor some day. You may have to hire legal representation to resolve matters.

Q: My bank, without telling me, raised its service charges on checking accounts. Aren't they supposed to give notice before implementing such a change?

A: Yes. Banks must give customers written notice of any changes in their account agreement. Most meet that requirement. Yours may have too without your being aware of it, as there are many inconspicuous ways the public disclosure requirement can be met. Good banks use a combination of methods ensuring all their customers are informed. Banks you shouldn't patronize meet the basic requirement as unobtrusively as possible and hope nobody notices.

Of course, if you're absolutely sure that your bank didn't inform you of the changes you should contact the appropriate banking authority.

Q: If my passbook is stolen, and someone makes a forged withdrawal, can I recover my funds?

A: Yes, under most circumstances. Just as with a checking account, a bank is obligated to know the signature of its depositors. If they paid a forgery they must return your money.

Q: Are Christmas clubs worth considering?

A: No. They are a packaging gimmick, as are most club accounts. Although there are many variances being offered, the basic premise is that you make fifty weekly deposits to save for a specific purpose. Many banks have the customer make the first forty-nine payments and the bank makes the last one as your "interest." Unfortunately, at some banks, if you miss one payment you lose your last payment, which means you have been saving for an interest rate return of 0 percent.

Other club accounts pay straight interest, but it's usually the lowest interest rate being offered by the bank for any of their accounts.

Regardless of how your bank's club accounts work, I can almost guarantee that if you put a pencil to it you'll find you could have earned more for your money using an alternative.

Q: My SuperNOW account advertises an interest rate of 7 percent, but has a minimum balance requirement of $2,500 or the interest rate lowers to the NOW account rate. My average service charge is $10 per month. How can I determine if this is a good deal?

A: Like all bank services, you have to shop before making a commitment. In this case you should be looking for the lowest possible minimum balance requirement. You also have to ascertain the net return on the account. For example, 7 percent on an average daily balance of $3,000 earns $17.50 per month. But you have to subtract your service charge of $10 to find the actual net interest rate return. In this case you're left with $7.50, or a return of only 3 percent.

SuperNOW accounts, even though they have a better return than NOW accounts, generally have a lower return than can be found in a money-market account. Of course, some money-market accounts have check writing restrictions, so you may have to weigh return against convenience before deciding the best account for your needs.

Q: I had a Time Certificate of Deposit mature. The bank never sent me a notice and then renewed it for another six months. Can they do that?

A: Yes. Unfortunately, banks have no obligation to notify customers that their TCD is maturing. Many TCD contract agreements have an inconspicuous and often overlooked notice stating that the bank can renew the funds for a like term if not notified to the contrary by the depositor prior to the grace period expiring.

Good banks close a matured TCD and send a check for the balance if they receive no instructions from the customer. Ask what your bank's renewal policy is before you invest.

General

Q: If my bank or savings and loan is closed, what happens to my money?

A: Assuming the institution is government insured, your deposits will be paid, in some manner, within ten days.

However, if the institution or industry is forced into a bank holiday you may have to wait an extended period of time before receiving your funds.

I have reservations regarding the government's guarantee. History makes clear that, whenever it deems necessary, the government will change the rules at our expense. In an actual financial industry collapse you can be assured the government guarantee will be greatly modified.

Q: My bank has a bill paying service that I use. What happens if they make a mistake?

A: You should bring the error to their attention immediately. They are obligated to fix it. If their negligence causes harm to your credit rating, or an added late charge or returned check expense, they have to bear the cost.

If great harm is done you may wish to bring a law suit for damages.

Q: I made a deposit to an Automated Teller Machine, but it didn't give me a receipt. What should I do?

A: As soon as possible you should contact the bank. They have to make a receipt available once they have had time to balance the machine for the day.

When something like this happens it's wise to start making notes outlining what time you made the deposit, what the deposit consisted of (for example, three twenty dollar bills, etc.), and any other information that may help the bank rectify matters.

Q: I made a deposit in the bank's night drop. Now they say they can't find it. What can I do?

A: Since a bank, rightfully, will not give you money based on nothing more than your word, you may have lost your deposit. Which is why I strongly recommend never making a deposit in a night drop, unless it consists totally of checks that you have signed with a restrictive endorsement. You can always get these checks replaced. That's not true for cash and unrestricted negotiable instruments.

Q: My bank offers brokerage services. They made a mistake in an order that cost me a great deal of money. Do I have any recourse?

A: Yes. Banks that provide brokerage services are obligated to the same standards as brokerage houses. If the bank will not respond positively to your complaint(s) you should contact the SEC (their address is in the Directory), in addition to reviewing matters with your attorney. Correspondence to the appropriate banking agencies would also be in order.

Whether it's travel, real estate, insurance, or brokerage services, when banks enter nontraditional markets they are obligated to comply with associated rules and regulations. This greatly expands your rights as a banking consumer.

Q: Can a bank's trust department be sued?

A: Absolutely. Any trustee, including a bank, can be sued for errors and mismanagement.

A lawyer specializing in trust matters should be contacted immediately if you believe a bank's trust department has acted contrary to your best interests.

Q: My bank prepares income taxes. If they make an error, what are my options?

A: The ultimate responsibility for any tax return belongs to the taxpayer, regardless of who prepared the return.

However, you may have civil recourse to collect monies lost if you can prove the bank did not meet the minimum standards for tax preparers and their error(s) caused additional obligations.

Q: I live in a small town. I know one of the bank's directors leaked information regarding my finances, and it's cost me money and reputation. Is there anything I can do?

A: Absolutely. Bank relationships are confidential in nature. If that confidentiality is inappropriately breached, in any harmful manner, by any of the bank's staff or management you have recourse.

Of course you have to be able to prove the connection between the breach and the bank and/or banker, and be able to prove damages. Unfortunately, too many bankers forget the confidential nature of their business. A substantial civil law suit will remind them.

Q: How can I find the least expensive bank credit card?

A: Write Bankcardholders of America, 560 Herndon Pkwy, #120, Herndon, VA 22070 (800/638-6407). For a small fee they provide an up-to-date listing of credit cards with the lowest interest rates, and/or they'll send a list of cards that have no annual fees.

Q: Are bank traveler's checks a good buy?

A: Not in my mind. First you're charged a fee to purchase the checks, and then the issuing bank or company gets to use your money as their investment float for as long as it takes the check(s) to clear. Because of the way traveler's checks are used—vacations, etc.—this is often an extended period of time.

Perhaps more important is the fact that traveler's checks are becoming obsolete, as major credit card companies now have nationwide networks of ATM's. Consequently, assuming you have a low-cost card that you use only for convenience, you have immediate comparatively inexpensive access to money without the high cost of traveler's checks.

Q: Now that banks are becoming involved in other areas, such as brokerage services, should I consider them?

A: I have reservations. Based on history, banks as an industry have given the public no reason to feel comfortable with the quality of their expertise. As time passes and current events unfold, our confidence level is being further eroded.

There may be some exceptions. Although I would recommend a national discount broker, I do understand those that have substantial proficiency in the stock market using a bank to place their orders.

That notwithstanding, as I don't recommend banking with

your travel agent, real estate broker, insurance agent, or tax preparer, I have qualms about doing the same in reverse. Use caution. As banks expand their services the consumer's exposure to risk is expanded proportionally.

Author's Note: None of my answers should be construed as a recommendation for a specific bank service. As is mentioned throughout the book, I believe that, in many cases, a bank does not compare favorably with other alternatives.

My responses are an acknowledgment that only a portion of my readers will have balanced their options between their bank and those alternatives. Others will continue to do all their financial business with their bank, regardless of what I say—these answers are offered so, if that's your choice, you can get the best deal possible.

Nontraditional Lending Sources for Small Businesses

In the section entitled "The Economics of Starting and Maintaining Your Own Business" (chapter 4) we discussed why standard bank financing for a small business may do far more harm than good. As I mentioned, there are many alternative sources available—the hardest part is knowing where to look. This listing will help.

1. *Private money:* These contacts can be made through your broker, accountant, venture capital clubs, lawyers, or an ad in the paper.

Private money likes a good return, which may make the borrowing costly. On the other hand, some private lenders offer rates substantially below the market. Regardless, their terms are usually liberal, which may be more important than rate.

Of course, you don't have to use a straight-loan scenario.

Stock and/or debentures can be used, which may limit the cost but escalate the lender's say in your business—a serious negative.

That notwithstanding, I recommend private money for almost any consumer or commercial loan, but urge attention to detail in structuring the relationship.

2. *Venture capital:* This money can be found through accountants, lawyers, financial advisors, and bankers.

These institutional-private lenders normally want a strong vested interest in a company. Therefore they commonly use a debt/equity structuring, which you may find difficult to live with. However, they have deep pockets, and are a source that must be considered when looking for substantial monies. I cannot overstate the necessity of caution with this source.

3. *Business development corporations (BDCs):* BDCs are private corporations chartered by state governments for the sole purpose of making loans to small businesses.

They are flexible in terms and often are overlooked by many because they aren't aware that they exist. Check your phone directory, and/or call your state capital's information operator. They will be able to direct you, provided that your state licenses BDCs.

These are private companies, so don't become lax and confuse their association with the state government. You're no safer here than with any other lender.

4. *State venture capital funds:* Approximately half the states have capital funds for small businesses. They are especially interested in new ventures, due to the obvious benefits that accrue to the state every time new jobs are created.

Call your state capital directory operator to see if your state has such a program. If so, they will direct your call.

This is an excellent source for funds if you're eligible. The plan is generally administered through the state's Industrial Development Commission.

5. *Incubators:* These are organizations set up by any number of associations. They can be sponsored in part or in whole by colleges, nonprofit organizations, etc.

They provide more services—such as shared office space, secretarial pools, executive assistance, and answering services—than they do money. As a company progresses, and no longer needs to share expenses for such services, it moves to its own quarters.

While the principal function of incubators is not providing lending, on occasion they do have their own investment pool, which they will loan under the proper circumstances. Additionally, they have access to many other organizations that do provide lending, which may be the lending link you need.

Locating incubators can be difficult. Call your state university's information office. They will give you a number to contact.

6. *Small Business Administration* (SBA): The SBA is normally thought of as the court-of-last-resort in the lending chain. Meaning they may make or assist loans that no traditional lender will make. However, the SBA should be one of your first thoughts as opposed to the last.

I don't like to recommend doing business with any government agency for a variety of well-founded reasons. However, in this case, provided you can stand the extra time and paperwork involved, the bottom line may be profitable. The rate saving, depending on the loan, may be substantial when applied to a large loan with extended terms. Then too, their terms can be extremely flexible. The bank funds the loan, but, since the SBA guarantees 90 percent of it, the bank's exposure to loss is minimal. Under those circumstances, favorable terms should be negotiable.

Suggestion: Shop your loan at institutions that have an SBA subdepartment in their loan department. Their sole purpose is to assist SBA applications. This will increase your chances of receiving approval, lessen your burden of paperwork, and perhaps offer options you are not presently aware of.

For a listing of institutions that have SBA departments, call the local SBA office listed in the phone book.

7. *Minority enterprise small business investment corporations* (MESBICs): A privately owned investment company licensed by the Small Business Administration for the sole purpose of assisting minorities in acquiring financing for their new business ventures.

Call your local SBA office for the name and number of the nearest MESBIC.

8. *Small business investment companies* (SBICs): A privately owned investment company licensed by the SBA for the sole purpose of assisting small businesses in acquiring lending for start-up or operating.

Call your local SBA office for the name and number of the SBICs located in your area.

Using traditional lending sources may make finding money difficult, expensive, and risky to a small business. However, my experience is that, provided you have a viable business concept, there is money available from any one of a number of nontraditional sources. Clearly, with all the alternatives, the local financial institution loses much of its luster. And that's a good thing. Looking elsewhere will save you money, in your business and personal finances, which is why this listing is offered.

Checking and Savings Alternatives

Checking and savings accounts are the most basic of banking services. However, as explored throughout the book, perhaps your bank isn't the best place to acquire those services. Here are some alternatives.

Checking

1. *Savings and loan associations* have lower service charges than most banks. Additionally, they have, on average, lower minimum balance requirements. As long as the institution is government insured, it's as "safe" as any bank.

2. *Credit unions* are another low-cost alternative. Their "checks," called draft shares, are often service-charge free. Those few that do service charge checking accounts have fees much lower than most banks. If they have a minimum balance requirement it is normally under $300. Their payment of checking account interest is generally one-half- to one-percentage point higher than banks pay. Not all credit unions have draft shares, so you may have to shop to find one in your area that does.

For help in locating a credit union you can join, call the Credit Union National Association at 800/356–9655.

3. *Service charge free accounts* are available at most banks. If you're under eighteen, retired, a student, disabled, or over sixty-five, ask if your bank will provide a checking account at no charge. Almost all banks, savings and loans, and credit unions provide this service—but it is seldom advertised or offered without being requested.

4. *Brokerage house accounts* offer, in addition to asset management, brokerage services, etc., checking account privileges at no or low charge. However, they may have a substantial fee to open the account, and/or a yearly fee to maintain it, so you have to balance your savings against the annual fees to see your true bottom line.

5. *Money market mutual funds* are another possibility, depending on your check writing needs. As many have a minimum dollar requirement, for example, each check must be written for at least $250, they may not meet your needs. If you can live with their prerequisites the cost is minimal.

6. *No-frills checking accounts* are offered by many banks and savings and loans. They have no minimum balance requirements, but often have a maximum on the number of checks you can write during a month. Your cost, provided you don't exceed the bank's activity limits, is a flat fee of approximately $2 to $5 per month. Each bank or savings and loan has its own particulars, so, as always, it pays to shop.

Savings

1. *Money market mutual funds,* in addition to possibly being your checking account alternative, have to be considered from a savings standpoint. If you want added safety with this account stick with those funds that invest only in Treasury bills.

2. *Tax-exempt money market funds* are an even better answer. Especially if you're in the higher income tax bracket. The effect of taxes cannot be ignored when investing in a savings vehicle. You may be able to lessen your state's income tax impact on your total tax obligation by investing in a tax-exempt money market fund that invests in municipal securities in your state. Lowering or negating your tax on an investment is worth investigating.

3. *Brokered TCD's,* while not necessarily good for the economic well-being of the country, are an excellent vehicle for maximizing your return. The broker shops rates nationwide and gets the best available that offers FDIC insurance. Brokered money contributed to the S&L crisis, but that's not germane, as it was a symptom not a cause. As long as you're dealing with a respectable broker, brokered TCD's can offer larger, substantially larger, returns than those offered at your local institutions.

4. *Treasury securities* are perhaps the safest consumer savings investment. The choice of vehicle is quite varied, from $25 savings bonds, Treasury notes and bills, to issues that require a minimum investment of $1 million.

Treasury investments can be purchased through your broker, most banks, or directly from the nearest Federal Reserve Bank. For a free booklet entitled "Marketable Treasury Securities," write: Federal Reserve Bank of Richmond, Public Services Dept., Box 27622, Richmond, VA 23261 (804/697-8109). *Buying Treasury Securities* is available for $4.50.

5. *Nonbank banks* have to be considered in today's aggressive market. Sears' Discover card account offers a savings plan, as does Household Financial Services, Beneficial Finance, and others. Credit unions also are also worthy of your consideration. Their rates are usually competitive and deposits are insured by the National Credit Union Share Insurance Fund.

(Note: This listing should not be thought of as all inclusive, but simply the starting point of your options. Investigate every opportunity. These are your safer choices. If your banking needs are substantially more sophisticated you may wish to consider a Swiss bank account, off-shore banking, private investments, etc.)

Glossary

Active Account   An account where deposits and withdrawals are made frequently.

Activity Charge   A service charge on a depositor's account (checking or savings). The amount of the charge(s) can vary greatly from bank to bank.

Administrator   An individual appointed by the court to settle the estate of someone who died without leaving a will.

Affiliate Bank   A bank whose management is closely related and/or associated with another bank.

American Banker's Association (ABA)   The ABA is the national organization of banks. Most commercial banks belong to the ABA. The ABA is the lobbying extension for the banking industry.

Amortization Loans   A term that applies to long-term loans (such as a mortgage) whereby the principal borrowed is paid off over the term of the loan (usually through monthly payments).

Appraisal The act of putting a value (fair market, sale, or loan value) on a piece of property (usually used in the context of real estate transactions).

Appraiser The person who performs the appraisal.

Appreciating Asset An asset that increases in value with the passage of time. A house, in most instances, is a perfect example of an appreciating asset.

Appreciation The increase in the value of property as compared to its cost at purchase.

Assets A term used to signify properties that have a value and are owned by an individual or business.

Authorized Capital Stock The number of shares of stock that a bank is authorized legally to issue.

Average Daily Balance The balance of an account added together every day for thirty days and then divided by thirty. This gives the financial institution a starting point when figuring its profitability on your account(s). It is also used to ascertain the amount of the monthly service fee the bank assesses your account(s).

Bad Debts Those accounts of the bank that are charged off due to delinquency. They represent an actual monetary loss of funds to the bank. Other circumstances, such as a bank accounting error, can also cause a bad debt for the bank.

Balloon Payment A lump-sum payment due in the future. Normally it is larger than the regular monthly payment. This type of payment is usually associated with mortgage lending.

Bank Account Money deposited in a bank. Generally, these are checking or some form of savings accounts.

Bank Auditors Persons hired by the bank to review the financial affairs of the institution. Bank auditors generally report directly to the board of directors.

Bank Balance The money deposited in a bank in your name that you are entitled to draw funds against.

Bank Bylaws   Rules that govern how an individual bank is managed. Such bylaws cannot be inconsistent with appropriate banking laws, civil and criminal law, or the bank's charter.

Bank Examiners   Persons appointed by law to examine and review the banking affairs of a financial institution. Banks are examined by either the state banking authority, the federal banking authority, and/or the Federal Deposit Insurance Corporation.

Bank Holiday   A time span during which banks are legally permitted to deny withdrawal requests by their depositors. Usually associated with the Great Depression, but have occurred more than once in the 1980s (in Ohio and Maryland).

Bank Lending Risk   The business risk faced by an institution that makes loans. The percentage of that risk is determined not by the borrowers, but by the lending expertise of the bank management team.

Bank Money Order   A negotiable instrument that is issued by a bank and paid for in advance by the customer. The cost is normally minimal.

Bankruptcy   A condition whereby an entity acknowledges that it cannot pay its debts. Further, liabilities exceed assets, so regardless of liquidation, a deficit will still exist.

Bank   A corporation legally organized to provide deposit facilities to the public (private or corporate).

Bank Stamp   The endorsement of a bank on the reverse side of a check. The stamp indicates legal acceptance and payment.

Bearer Instrument   Any ownership document that is payable legally to the "Bearer," that is, it indicates no specific party or payee. The owner is the person who is in possession.

Beneficiary   The person for whose benefit a specific trust account operates.

Billion   A thousand millions.

Blank Endorsement   An endorsement with no specific payee. Consequently, it may legally be paid by signature to the bearer.

Bond   A contractual agreement representing a loan for a specific amount and term. The party that buys the bond is the lender. The party selling the bond is the borrower. In most cases they are bought at face value, discount, or premium.

Book Value   The value of bank stock as shown by the institution's records. This is the bank's total capital stock, capital surplus, undivided profits, and legal reserves divided by the number of outstanding bank shares.

Branch Banking   The system of banking that allows a bank to do business in multiple locations other than its main office. While some states do not allow branch banking, the "unit bank state" is disappearing rapidly. Banking across state lines is now commonplace. Many fear that this expansion of a bank's influence is placing too much of the nation's wealth in the hands of fewer and fewer bankers.

Call Loan   A loan that can be presented for payment at any time by the lender. Obviously a dangerous way to borrow money under most circumstances.

Call Report   The statement of condition of a bank. It is prepared by order of the appropriate banking authority. A condensed version of the report must be published in a local newspaper.

Cancelled Check   A check received with your monthly statement, and which has been paid and cancelled by the bank. Many institutions, to lower their costs, no longer send cancelled checks back to the customer.

Capital and Surplus   A condensed accounting indicating a bank's financial strength. Comprised of the bank's capital, surplus, undivided profits, and reserve accounts.

Capital Stock   Bank stock that has been issued in return for payment of investment money from its shareholders.

Cashier's Check   A bank check that can be purchased by any bank consumer. That check is a direct obligation of the bank and is generally assumed to mean that payment is guaranteed.

Cash Items   Checks, etc., that are deposited for immediate credit but are subject to reversal against your account should they be returned for any reason.

Certificate of Deposit (CD)   A receipt for a deposit either payable on demand or at a specific date in the future. Normally the CD—also called a Time Certificate of Deposit (TCD)—is for a certain amount of money, at a certain interest rate, maturing at a specific date, and is a negotiable instrument.

Certified Check   A check that guarantees that the signature of the drawer is genuine and there are sufficient funds on deposit to ensure payment. Payment cannot be denied for lack of funds, and once a bank certifies a check it becomes a bank obligation even though it is drawn on a customer's account.

Check   A negotiable instrument drawn on a bank and payable on demand.

Checking Account   An account against which checks may be drawn.

Christmas Club   A savings account with weekly deposits, the balance of which is payable in December. Many banks have numerous club accounts for varying purposes. In most cases, because of the interest computations of these types of accounts, the customer would be better off saving through a standard individual account.

Collateralized Assets   The assets pledged by the borrower for the purpose of meeting the security requirements as outlined by the lender.

Collateral Loan   A loan for which the borrower has pledged asset security. The collateral may be sold by the lender if the loan terms are not met.

Collected Balance   The actual balance in an account that the bank has been paid for. The collected balance in an account is normally less than the actual balance. Using the Expedited Funds Availability Act criterion, banks withhold payment to an account for a specified period of time even though they have been paid for the deposit items. This creates bank float, allowing the bank the maximum use of your funds.

Collection Items   Checks deposited in a bank for which the customer receives credit only when the item has been directly paid for by the payee bank. This is accomplished through separate channels and not through normal clearing procedures.

Common Stock   Common stock represents the last claim on assets.

Compensating Balances   Deposits in a checking account that a bank requires for approval on certain business loan applications. Usually 10 to 30 percent of the outstanding loan balance. A requirement by banks to maximize their loan incomes.

Compound Interest   Interest paid on principal and accumulated (not withdrawn) interest previously earned.

Cost of Money   The interest rate customers pay for the privilege of borrowing money. Or, for the bank, the cost of acquiring deposits. In a universal sense this cost is controlled by the Federal Reserve, "the banker's bank."

Note: Fed banks act as distribution points for currency, which is then used by the banking community. The Fed's discount interest rate is normally the starting point for the setting of interest rates in the private sector. The true power of the Federal Reserve is virtually unknown by the general public. In truth, our economy and our monetary system are controlled by a handful of unelected bankers. In terms of real economic power, the Fed and the Federal Reserve chairman are more powerful than the president, Congress, and the Supreme Court combined.

Counter Check   A check available to bank customers that takes the place of their own checks.

Custodial Account   Any account whereby one takes possession of another's assets. The customer (in a bank context) retains ownership of the account's value.

Debenture   Bonds issued by a bank that are not secured by any specific bank asset.

Defalcation   The illegal appropriation (embezzlement) by a bank employee of bank money or property, or that of its depositors.

Default   The failure to meet the terms of a lending contract, that is, nonpayment.

Demand Deposits   Deposits subject to checks that can be withdrawn immediately. For example, a checking account.

Demand Loan   A loan that is payable on demand by the lender. Another term for a call loan.

Deposits   Money owed by the bank to its depositors.

Depreciation   The decrease in the value of property as compared to cost.

Depression   Usually caused by a shortage of money or by high-priced credit. Sometimes both are in evidence. This causes economic inactivity, which further exacerbates the condition.

Devaluation   Lowering the value of a country's currency. The most memorable example of devaluation was Germany in the early 1900s. Many believe that the United States may have no choice, due to its debt structure, but to opt for some form of devaluation in the forseeable future.

Directors   The individuals who have the direct responsibility of bank management.

Dividend   A proportionate distribution of a bank's yearly earnings paid to the shareholders of record.

Dormant Account   A bank account with little or no activity over a predetermined period of time. Many banks now charge a monthly fee for those accounts (checking and savings) that are inactive during the month, regardless of the account's balance.

Draft   A negotiable instrument payable on acceptance, unlike a check, which is payable on demand.

Drawee   The bank at which a check is expected to be paid.

Drawer   The person who makes out a check.

Earnings per Share   The bank's yearly earnings divided by the number of shares of stock outstanding.

Embezzlement   The illegal appropriation of money entrusted to a bank.

Endorsement   The writing by the payee on the back of a negotiable instrument (usually a check). The signature passes title to another.

Equity   The difference between the sale value of a property and the amount still owed on said property.

Executor   A person appointed through a will to carry out the financial wishes of the deceased.

FDIC   Federal Deposit Insurance Corporation. An executive agency that insures deposits for all banks entitled to FDIC insurance.

Federal Debt   The total amount of monies owed by the federal government to its creditors.

Federal Debt Limit   The limit of federal debt as allowed by law. This limit has no practical meaning anymore, as Congress simply increases it whenever it deems necessary. Instead of being the restraining vehicle it was intended to be, the debt limit has become a visible reminder of the financial inabilities of our legislators.

Federal Deficit   The yearly shortfalls between the money the government takes in and the money it spends. This difference is compensated for by additional borrowing, which then increases the problem through added debt service.

Federal Funds Funds on deposit with the Federal Reserve by member banks. This is the banking industry's daily investment pool.

Federal Reserve Bank Any one of the twelve Federal Reserve banks.

Fiat Money Money declared to be legal by a government. Said currency is not convertible to gold, silver, or any other commodity. Its value is entirely based on the faith of its users.

Fiduciary A person or corporation that is entrusted with the property of another.

FIFO An acronym meaning First-In-First-Out. When compounding interest using FIFO, the bank considers any withdrawals to have come out of the earliest deposit or balance during the interest period. This is costly to consumers and lowers their net interest returns, while returning more to the bank.

Financial Statement A balance sheet, or statement of condition. Can be prepared for business or personal use.

First Lien The first claim right against a property, such as a home or other pledged security.

Fiscal Policy The guidelines and policies that represent the monetary policy of the country. In effect it becomes the budgetary policy of the government.

Float Deposited funds that receive immediate credit but have yet to be collected. With the advent of deposit "hold time," depositor float is virtually nonexistent. On the other hand, since the hold times are not consistent with actual collection times, bank float has become one of the bank's most profitable income producers.

Foreclosure Action taken by a lender when the conditions of the mortgage have not been met. The mortgage holder may institute proceedings to force the owner to pay the mortgage in full and/or sell the property.

Forged Negotiable Instrument   Checks, etc., that have had the maker's or payee's signature(s) falsified. Also applies to any document alteration for the purpose of defrauding.

Free Market   A market regulated by competition rather than by government. Our economy is referred to as a free market, but of course that's not the case.

Garnishment   A process authorizing a financial institution to impound monies on deposit for the purpose of paying another legal debt. The bank awaits a court order before forwarding any money.

Guarantee   A promise to pay in case of default of a lending debt.

Guarantor   A person who guarantees payment of a loan. The guarantor may or may not receive any benefit from the loan's proceeds.

Guardian   A person who has the legal right to control a minor and/or the estate of another.

Holder in Due Course   A person who accepts a negotiable instrument for value, in good faith, and without prior knowledge that the instrument is defective in any way. A holder in due course is normally protected from any legal claims arising from dishonor or refusal to pay.

Hold Time   The time limit a bank declares is necessary before it will allow a depositor to draw against funds deposited. During this time limit the bank may or may not pay you interest for those deposits.

Inactive Account   A bank account that has little or no activity. These accounts are usually isolated from active accounts and then assessed monthly bank fees. Depending on state laws, the bank often remits the balance to the state revenue agency after the passage of five to ten years. The rightful owner of the account can always redeem the funds from the state by proving ownership.

Inflation   The devaluation of money. Usually caused by continual, uncontrolled private and government debt. In effect, it becomes a "tax" we can't keep up with.

Installment Loan   A loan in which the borrower pays a portion of the value of the loan every month until the amount owed is completely paid back.

Insufficient Funds   The return of a check because the depositor does not have a sufficient balance to allow payment.

Interest   The rental cost of money paid by a bank to its savings depositors. Or, in a lending context, the rental cost of money paid by borrowers to a bank.

Interlocking Directors   Directors of one bank who are also directors of another bank or banks.

Joint Account   A bank account owned by two or more persons. Unless otherwise contracted, each has deposit and withdrawal rights.

Joint Tenancy   Property owned by two or more persons.

Junior Mortgage   A lower-ranking mortgage, as opposed to a first mortgage. There may be numerous junior mortgages on a property. Claims against the property are settled in order, that is, first mortgage, second mortgage, third mortgage, and so on.

Kiting   The raising of fraudulent account balances on uncollected funds among a number of financial institutions. Check kiting is a criminal offense.

Legal Tender   Any form of currency or money that must be legally accepted as payment for a debt.

Liabilities   The monetary obligations of a business or individual, that is, what you must pay.

Lien   A hold or claim against the property of another as security for a loan or other obligation.

LIFO   An acronym meaning Last-In-First-Out. In compound-

ing interest using LIFO, the bank considers any withdrawal to come out of the latest deposit or balance during
the interest period. This is better than FIFO interest, but
not as good as day-of-deposit-to-day-of-withdrawal interest, compounded and paid daily.

Line of Credit   The maximum prior approved dollar amount
that a specific person can borrow from his or her bank. In
effect, a preapproved loan.

Liquid Assets   Current assets that can immediately be
turned into cash.

Liquidation   The selling of an asset.

Loans   The renting of money. Usually to be repaid with interest.

Lost Passbook   Since a passbook is only a memorandum of
deposits, this is not a serious problem. A lost passbook
should be reported to the bank immediately, however, to
lessen your inconvenience and any loss to the bank.

Maker   A person who makes out a check.

Market Value   The present salable value of a property.

Maturity   The due date of an obligation.

Million   A thousand thousands.

Minimum Free Balance   The minimum account balance the
bank requires in an account for the account not to be
charged a service fee.

Minutes   The written proceedings of a shareholders' or
board of directors' meeting.

Monetary Authority   The Constitution vests the power for
creating money with Congress. It allows our representatives to create fiat money at their discretion. The advisability of fiat money, and the manner in which Congress uses
its monetary authority, has long been debated.

Money   A medium of exchange.

Money Market   In an educational context, the supply of
funds and the demand for said funds. In a general sense,

another definition would be a money market fund.

Mortgage A document conveying title to land that is used for collateral.

Negotiable Instrument Orders to pay money. A check is a negotiable instrument.

Net Worth The value of an estate or business after deducting all outstanding liabilities. A negative net worth exists when obligations exceed assets.

Note A document indicating a debt and agreed-upon promise to pay.

NSF An acronym meaning nonsufficient funds.

Obligor A person who owes money.

Overdraft An account on the books of the bank that indicates the total balance of all accounts that are presently overdrawn. On a specific account it indicates that the owner has paid out in excess of his or her deposits.

Overextension A condition whereby a person has more debt than he or she can possibly be expected to repay.

Par Value The face value of an instrument.

Passbook A book that records banking deposits and withdrawals.

Payee The person to whom a check is made payable.

Personal Check A check written on the account of an individual as opposed to the account of a business.

Personal Property All nonreal property owned by an individual.

Portfolio All the investments, expressed as a total, of a person or corporation.

Postdated Check A check that bears a date in the future, as opposed to the date on which it was written.

Power of Attorney A document that allows one individual to act on behalf of another. A power of attorney can be for a specific transaction or all legal transactions depending on the intent of the grantor.

Prime Rate   The lending interest rate the banks charge their best commercial customers. This is the banker's definition.

Principal   The amount of a debt that interest is computed on.

Promissory Note   A note that indicates that a person or entity will pay a certain sum of money on a certain future date.

Purchasing Power   An expression of the value of money as it pertains to goods and services. Since fiat money has no intrinsic value, purchasing power is an important benchmark, as it assigns a value to the dollar.

Real Estate   Real property.

Recession   A decline in business activity. Usually caused by monetary shortages, and can sometimes be the prelude to the more severe problem of depression.

Refer to Maker   A method of returning a check that forces the payee to ask the maker why the check was not paid. It's the bank's way of not becoming involved in the transaction and/or not embarrassing the maker by sending the check back NSF.

Renewal   The extension of a loan by allowing the customer to pay off the old note with the proceeds of a new note.

Repurchase Agreement   A note sold by a bank, with the obligation/promise to repurchase it at a later date.

Returned Item   A check returned from the drawee bank to the presenting bank. There are varying reasons for such a return, that is, missing endorsement, NSF, alterations, postdated requirement, etc.

Rule of 78s   The formula whereby a bank can accelerate consumer installment loan interest into its profit accounts prior to when it is actually owed.

Savings Accounts   Funds on deposit at a bank that are not subject to check withdrawal and are paid interest.

Savings Banks   Banks which specialize in and promote savings by individuals.

Second Mortgage A mortgage placed on property that already has a first mortgage on it.

Secured Loan A loan where the borrower pledges collateral to the lender in case of default.

Security Loan collateral.

Short-Term Loans Loans that will mature within one year.

Sight Draft A negotiable instrument payable on presentation (assuming all contractual aspects of the draft can be met).

Signatures A bank is obligated by law to know the signatures of its depositors and is liable if it pays any negotiable instrument that has been forged on their customer's accounts.

Single Payment, Simple Interest Note Unlike an installment loan that charges interest on the original balance throughout the term of the loan, single payment, simple interest notes charge the consumer interest for the balance at any point in time. This is the best loan vehicle for the average family to borrow money.

Speculation An investment made solely on the anticipation of profits being made from a change of price as opposed to dividends or interest returns. Speculation involves more than normal risk taking.

Statement of Account A record prepared by the bank and sent to the customer outlining all account transactions during the month.

Stock Certificate A certificate of stock ownership.

Stockholder The owner of one or more shares of (bank) stock.

Stop Payment The order to a bank not to honor a specific negotiable instrument. If the bank misses a stop-payment order (assuming the order contained correct information and was presented in time to give the bank sufficient time to process same) it must reimburse the depositor for the amount of the check.

Tax   A payment, usually in currency, collected by a government. An individual may or may not be willing to pay the tax, but that's moot, as the fundamental premise of taxing is the government's ability to force compliance.

Teller   A banker who accepts deposits and honors withdrawals.

Third Mortgage   A mortgage placed on property that already has a first and second lien on it.

Time Deposit   Deposits due a customer at a future date. This is a form of savings account and has many differing forms. Interest rates are based on the length of the contract between the customer and bank.

Title   Documented proof that a person or entity is the rightful owner of a specific piece of property.

Traveler's Checks   Prepaid checks, sold by a bank, that normally are honored worldwide. In most cases the bank is just a middleman and the checks are actually drawn on a different corporation. In addition to the fee involved, the corporation creates huge float for its own investment purposes, as the checks may take months to clear back to the issuing bank.

Treasury Bills   Non–interest bearing, discounted notes issued by the U.S. government. They are redeemed at face value.

Trillion   A thousand billions.

Trust   The supervision of property so an individual may benefit from the resulting income.

Trust Department   The bank department that transacts trust business.

Trustee   The person or entity to whom a trust is commended.

Unencumbered   Property free of all liability claims.

Unsecured Loan   A loan not having security (collateral).

U.S. Government Securities   Financial obligations of the United States government. These can take varying forms and are issued by many different government agencies and departments.

Usury   A loan interest rate in excess of the legal maximum.

Wealth   A measurement of usable resources.

Wire Transfer   The transfer of money verbally as opposed to by instrument. This is the fastest and safest way to get monies from one financial institution to another.

Contacting the Author

To reach me with any comments, questions, or consulting needs, write Reliance Enterprises, Inc., P.O. Box 413, Marengo, IL 60152.

I would also like to respectfully recommend that you consider a subscription to my newsletter. *Money Insider* is dedicated to giving you the confidential information your banker, stockbroker, lawyer, and others don't want you to have. I know you'll be pleased with the uniqueness of our format, the value of our market counsel, and the immediate benefit of each article.

If you would like to review a free issue, send a business-size SASE and $2 for handling to Reliance at the address above. To subscribe, send $49 for twelve monthly issues to *Money Insider*, P.O. Box 12269, Boulder, CO 80303-0070.